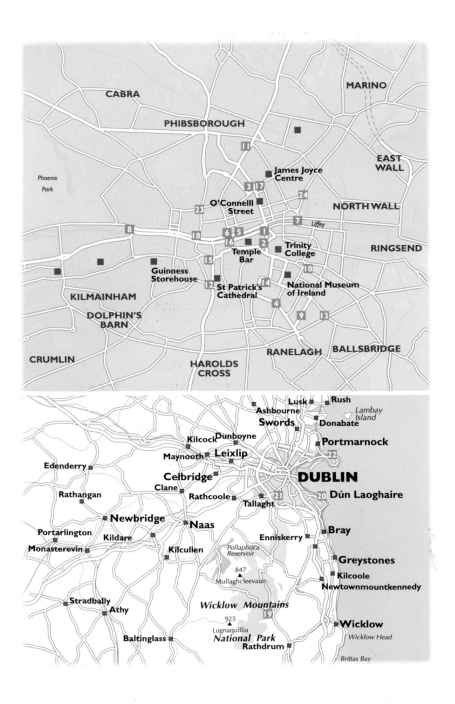

# CONTENTS

# Introduction

Hidden histories and mysteries leap out at every turn of Dublin's streets. Ireland's capital is one of the oldest cities in Europe, founded by Vikings and home to artists, poets, authors and rebels for more than 1,000 years. Grand public buildings, squares of elegant Georgian townhouses, grim jails, churches and cathedrals hark back to the heyday of the British ascendancy, centuries-old pubs lurk on cobbled streets, and statues commemorate heroes, villains, mythical figures and great literary names. Through it all flows the River Liffey, source of the key ingredient of what Dubliners will affirm is the world's greatest pint. All of this comes in one compact package, eminently suitable for exploring on foot. Dublin has depth, but it's still a small and walker-friendly city.

Its roots go back to the glory days of the Vikings, who sailed through the mists of the Irish Sea to carve out a settlement on the shores of Dublin Bay in the 9th century AD. The Vikings were still there two centuries later, though by then they had turned Christian and acquired a brood of Irish in-laws. Next came the Normans, land-hungry as ever, ushering in almost nine centuries of British occupation and Irish rebellion against it. From the original Viking settlement on the banks of the Liffey, Dublin grew first into a medieval city around its castle and cathedral, then ultimately into a grand 18th- and 19th-century metropolis. In the 20th century it grew still further, especially since membership of the European Union boosted Ireland's economy so that it became known as the 'Celtic Tiger'. Today it's a city that looks to the future rather than the past, but that past still lurks at seemingly every corner. If you're willing to put on your walking shoes and look beyond the 21st-century Dublin of designer stores, espresso bars, boutique hotels and ultra-trendy bars and clubs, the ghosts of saints, sinners, scientists, satirists and swordsmen are waiting to greet you.

The walks contained in this book reflect every aspect of Dublin. They take in purpose-built visitor attractions that celebrate Dublin's past; grand public buildings and poky pubs; Liffey bridges and Georgian crescents. On the way you'll meet statues of great authors, playwrights, poets and political titans and catch a breath of

fresh air in landscaped gardens and grand parks.

So which are Dublin's unmissable itineraries? The answer is, of course, all of them. But if your time is limited, Walk 2 will give you a taste of the temple of learning that is Trinity College; Walk 6 will take you around Dublin's grandest medieval buildings; Walk 12 will lead you in the footsteps of some of its greatest men of letters; and Walk 24 will give you a sample of vibrant, trendy 21st-century Dublin.

Take your time as you soak up Dublin's stories and pause for a pint whenever you feel like it. The city can't be seen in a day, and every old street has a story to tell. So, of course, does every Dubliner, and you may well find yourself being regaled with more tales of hidden histories than you will find in this book. You can visit Dublin at any time of year. Winter temperatures rarely drop below 50°F (10°C), and in summer the mercury rarely rises much above 70°F (21°C), so there's good walking weather all year round. That said, the best season to visit is really summer and early autumn (from mid-May to mid-September), when the weather is mostly mellow enough to make walking (and sitting outdoors) a pleasure. Bear in mind that it can and does rain – often heavily – at any time of year. On the walks in this book, you're never far from shelter, but a waterproof jacket, watertight footwear, a hat and an umbrella are essential kit.

## WHERE TO EAT

| € | = | Inexpensive |
| €€ | = | Moderate |
| €€€ | = | Expensive |

ABOVE: HA'PENNY BRIDGE OVER THE RIVER LIFFEY

# The Uncrowned Kings of Ireland

**This walk introduces you to two of the greatest figures of Ireland's 19th-century history, Daniel O'Connell and Charles Stuart Parnell.**

One of the titans of Ireland's independence struggle stands guard over the street that bears his name, and O'Connell Street is lined with mementoes of Irish heroes and martyrs, including the battle-scarred façade of the General Post Office where a garrison of freedom fighters held out for six days against the guns of the British Army during the Easter Rising of 1916. Though it failed to inspire the popular revolt its leaders had hoped for, the harsh measures taken by the British after the rising created a huge groundswell of support for the Republican movement, culminating in the creation six years later of the first Irish Free State. At the very beginning of this walk there are great views up and down the River Liffey, which flows from west to east through the city centre, dividing Dublin in two. At the north end of O'Connell Street, at its intersection with Parnell Street, stands a monument to another legendary campaigner in the cause of Irish independence.

From the bus stop next to the River Liffey, at the corner of D'Olier Street and Burgh Quay, turn about to face the river and walk north across O'Connell Bridge. On your right, downriver, is the great copper dome of the Custom House, crowned by an allegorical bronze statue of Commerce. On your left, upriver, is the Liffey Bridge, commonly known as Ha'penny Bridge because when it was built in 1816 a halfpenny was charged to walk across it.

Ahead of you, at the foot of O'Connell Street on the left, a statue of Daniel O'Connell, 'the Liberator' (1775–1847), dominates the proceedings. O'Connell was the first great non-violent agitator against the Union of Britain and Ireland. Though a fiery orator, he advocated peaceful mass protest in place of violent resistance to British rule, and condemned the rebellion of 1803 led by Robert Emmett. Elected to the Irish Parliament in 1828, O'Connell was barred from taking his place as an MP because of his Catholic faith. The mass protests that followed led in 1829 to the Emancipation Act, allowing the election of Catholics. In 1841 he became the first Catholic mayor of Dublin. In 1843, now almost 70 years old, he was convicted of conspiracy and jailed for a year after calling a huge rally to demand repeal of the Union. Though released after three months, O'Connell became deeply disenchanted at the failure of his life-long campaign of peaceful opposition. A sick man, he left Dublin for sunnier Italy in 1847, but died soon after arriving in Genoa. The foundation stone

of the statue was laid two years before his death, but the statue itself, by John Foley, was not finally unveiled until 1864.

2 Leaving the statue behind, carry on up the left-hand side of O'Connell Street to the corner of Abbey Street Middle. Cross Abbey Street, and just on your right is a statue to a hero of the international trade union movement and the Left in Ireland.

James 'Big Jim' Larkin (1874–1947) was born of Irish parents in Liverpool and grew up in the city's slums. A dockworker and trade union activist, he came to Dublin in 1908 to set up the Irish Transport and General Workers' Union (ITGWU). In 1913 he led a long and bitter dispute with the Dublin United Tramway Company after its owner tried to break the union by sacking its members. After seven months, the strikers

9

OPPOSITE: O'CONNELL BRIDGE; ABOVE: JAMES LARKIN STATUE

DISTANCE **0.9 miles (1.5km)**

ALLOW **45 minutes**

START **South side of O'Connell Bridge**

FINISH **Corner of O'Connell Street and Parnell Street**

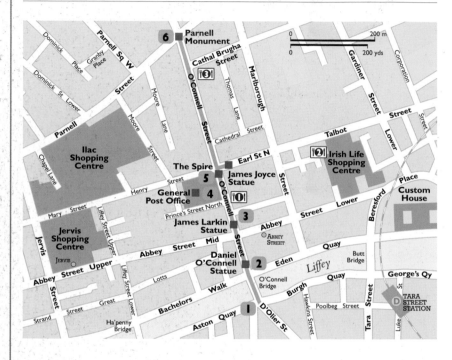

were forced to return to work, but their action became a landmark in the history of organized labour in Ireland. Larkin left for the US, where he became a keen supporter of the new Union of Soviet Socialist Republics and was sentenced to five years in jail on trumped-up charges of 'criminal anarchy'. Deported from the US, he returned to Ireland in 1923 and set up the communist Irish Workers' League. In 1927 he became the first communist to be elected to the Dáil (lower house of Parliament). He moved away from

Soviet-style communism, but he remained a man of the Left until his death in 1947. On the plinth of his statue, erected in 1980, is a quote (in French, Irish and English) from one of his speeches: 'The great appear great only because we are on our knees. Let us rise.' The slogan and the sentiment are borrowed from Camille Demoulins, one of the firebrands of the French Revolution.

**3** Continue along the left-hand side of O'Connell Street for one short

OPPOSITE: 'THE SPIKE' OUTSIDE THE GENERAL POST OFFICE

block. Immediately after crossing Princes Street North, on your left is the grandiose façade of the General Post Office. Look closely, and you can still see the scars left by British bullets and shells during the Easter Rising of 1916. Turn left, through the imposing portico designed by Francis Johnson in 1818 and topped by a statue of Mercury, courier of the gods, into the main hall of the building.

A statue of Cúchulainn, the warrior-hero of ancient Irish legends, stands in the main hall, symbolizing the Irish Volunteers who held out for six days here during the ill-fated rising. Their leaders, James Connolly and Padraig Pearse,

hoped that direct-armed action would inspire a broader mass insurrection, but Dubliners stayed indoors while British forces shelled the rebels into submission. The nationalists lost 64 dead and killed 130 British troops. The real victims, however, were the people of Dublin: some 300 civilians died in the fighting. Pearse, Connolly and other ringleaders were sentenced to die by firing squad – an act of vengeance that turned them into Republican martyrs.

4 Turn left out of the Post Office and carry on up O'Connell Street, where a vast obelisk of gleaming steel has been in view since you began this walk.

Officially called the Monument of Light (*An Tur Solais* in Irish), more generally known as the Spire of Dublin and irreverently nicknamed 'the Spike', this 390ft (120m) construction is claimed to be the world's tallest sculpture. Commissioned in 1999 and completed in 2003, it stands on the site of the Nelson Pillar, a stone column erected in honour of the famed British admiral and blown up in 1966 by a breakaway Republican group who felt that this hero of the British Empire no longer deserved such a prominent position in the capital of the Irish Republic.

5 Cross O'Connell Street, leave the Spire on your left, and turn right into Earl Street North. At the corner of this pedestrian street, outside the Café Kylemore, stands a debonair, larger-than-life statue.

JAMES JOYCE STATUE

Bespectacled, hands in pockets, legs crossed and hat at a jaunty angle, this is James Joyce (1882–1941), the author whose work is most closely associated with Dublin. He drew on his native city for inspiration, but left Dublin in 1904, at the age of 22, living in self-imposed exile in Trieste, Paris and Zurich, where he died in 1941. During that time he returned only for a few brief visits. But this has not stopped Dublin making the most of its connection with the great man. Sculpted by Marjorie Fitzgibbon, the statue was erected in 1990.

**6** Carry on up the right-hand side of O'Connell Street for three blocks, crossing Earl Street North, Cathedral Street and Cathal Brugha Street, to the north end of O'Connell Street. In the middle of the crossroads where O'Connell Street meets Parnell Street stands an imposing marble monolith, the Parnell Monument.

Nicknamed 'the uncrowned King of Ireland' – a soubriquet also applied to Daniel O'Connell 30 years earlier – Charles Stuart Parnell (1846–91) ranks alongside O'Connell as one of the titans of Ireland's struggle for Home Rule. Through his political agitation and demands for land reform, Parnell built a strong movement for home rule for Ireland, but his fragile political alliance with the Liberal government of William Gladstone was damaged by the murder of the British Chief Secretary for Ireland, Fredrick Cavendish, by the extremist 'Invincibles', and in 1890 his credibility

with his own party was destroyed by the revelation of his affair with a married woman, Katharine O'Shea, when her husband cited him as co-respondent in their divorce. Parnell died the following year, after marrying Katharine. He was only 45. Buses 40, 40A and 40B stop on either side of Parnell Street, a few yards to the right of the crossroads and the Parnell Monument.

## WHERE TO EAT

**CLERY'S,**
11–27 O'Connell Street;
Tel: 878 6000.
The smart café of one of Dublin's main department stores serves light lunches and substantial afternoon teas. €

**101 TALBOT STREET,**
100–102 Talbot Street;
Tel: 874 5011.
An excellent vegetarian menu along with substantial offerings for carnivores; there is a pasta bar in addition to the main restaurant and this is a better choice for a quick bite. €/€€

**GRESHAM HOTEL,**
23 O'Connell Street;
Tel: 874 6881.
Choose the main restaurant for a lavish à la carte lunch, but if you arrive here in the afternoon the Gresham also serves an excellent afternoon tea. €€€

# Age of Ascendancy

**Following in the footsteps of Dublin's celebrated figures, this walk leads you on a collegiate ramble through four centuries of academic excellence.**

Trinity College is one of Dublin's oldest and most august buildings and the alma mater of some of its most famous sons – among them Jonathan Swift, Oliver Goldsmith and Samuel Beckett. Founded in 1592, during the reign of English Queen Elizabeth I, it remained solely Protestant – in an overwhelmingly Catholic country – until the first Catholic students were enrolled in the 1970s. Until Ireland gained its independence, Trinity, the finest educational establishment in Ireland, excluded Catholics, and indeed the university's original mission was to provide the sons of the Protestant ruling class with an excellent education in Ireland, thus keeping them from falling into the snares of the Catholic universities of France or Italy. Ironically, after independence, it was the renascent and domineering Roman Catholic Church that prohibited students from Catholic families from aspiring to an education here. Happily, Trinity now attracts students from all over the world, and its immaculate quadrangles are open to everyone.

The west side of College Green is dominated by the grand Palladian façade of the Bank of Ireland. Enter the building through the grand portico in front, giving a nod as you pass to the statue that stands there.

The statue is of Henry Grattan (1746–1820), the leader of the Irish Parliament that in 1782 passed the Declaration of Rights empowering Roman Catholics to become practising lawyers, and also calling for independence for Ireland. His timing was unfortunate. Britain had just lost its American colonies, and was in no mood to concede anything to Ireland. When it was completed in 1739, the dignified building was the world's first purpose-built parliament house, but served its original purpose for less than a century. The Irish Parliament became a platform for spokesmen like Grattan, but in 1800 the British government forced the Act of Union, making the Dublin parliament redundant. The Bank of Ireland bought the building soon afterwards, and added more prosaic sections, converting the former House of Commons into its cash office. Join one of the guided tours of the former House of Lords, with its splendid wood-panelled interior. The huge tapestries that celebrate the great victories of the Protestant Ascendancy in 1690 at the Siege of Londonderry and the Battle of the Boyne seem oddly out of place in 21st-century Dublin.

2 Leave the bank, about face, and cross College Green to the main entrance of Trinity College. The college's

## WHERE TO EAT

[1O1] BANK,
20–22 College Green;
Tel: 677 0677.
www.bankoncollegegreen.com
A good place to start a day's walking as it opens at 9am and serves a full Irish breakfast. €€

[1O2] THE BANKERS,
16 Trinity Street;
Tel: 679 3697.
Traditional pub favoured by students, serving bar meals, snacks and an excellent pint. €

[1O3] JACOB'S LADDER,
4 Nassau Street;
Tel: 670 3865.
www.jacobsladder.ie
Chef Adrian Roche specializes in modern Irish cuisine with signature dishes such as pigeon cooked three ways and shellfish coddle. €€€

dignified grey stone façade, the West Front, occupies the block facing you.

A semicircular lawn, College Green, lies in front of the main entrance and provides the setting for statues of two of Trinity's most famous alumni. To the left, as you face the entrance, stands Edmund Burke (1729–97), the conservative philosopher and outspoken opponent of the French Revolution. On your right is Oliver Goldsmith (1738–74), the 18th-century satirist and playwright.

DISTANCE **0.25 mile (400m)**

ALLOW **2 hours**

START **College Green**

FINISH **Nassau Street**

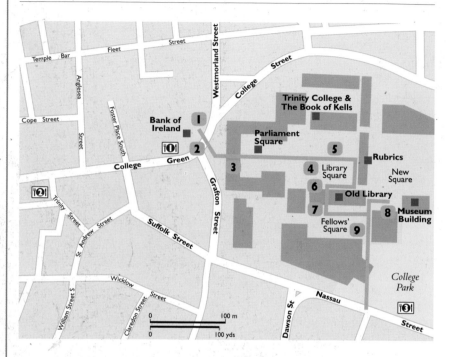

**3** Pass through the grand wood-panelled main entrance into a cobbled quadrangle, which has well-manicured lawns to either side. This is still known as Parliament Square, and ahead of you stands one of Trinity's most prominent landmarks.

The Campanile, a 100ft (30m) tall bell tower, stands on the site of the much older Augustinian monastery of All Hallows, which was dissolved by Elizabeth I's father, Henry VIII, during the turbulent years of the Reformation. This stolid, solid building was designed by Sir Charles Lanyon (who also designed Queen's University, Belfast) and was built in 1853. The bell tower stands atop an arched base; walk through the arch, and on your left is one of Trinity's more modern landmarks, a massive abstract sculpture. *Reclining Connected Forms* (1969) is unmistakably the work of Henry Moore, whose sculptures grace the great parks of so many world cities.

OPPOSITE: A PAGE FROM THE BOOK OF KELLS

**4** You are now on Library Square, and facing you (occupying the entire east side of the square) is an imposing four-storey, redbrick façade.

Although Trinity was founded in 1592, this building, known as the Rubrics and dating from about 1700, is the oldest extant part of the college complex.

**5** With the Campanile behind you, walk between the lawns of Library Square. Just in front of the Rubrics, turn right, and at the corner of the square turn right again. On your left now you will see the rear of the Old Library. Continue to the end of the building, turn left and left again and walk halfway down the front of the Old Library (the south side of Fellows' Square) to its entrance, on your left.

The Old Library, which took 20 years to build (from 1712 to 1732) is the most impressively gracious element of Trinity College's architectural treasury, and its splendid, echoing Long Room, with its towering oak shelves holding more than 200,000 volumes, is an amazing storehouse of knowledge. Like the British Library in London, the Old Library has the right to a copy of each and every book published in the UK and the Republic of Ireland (including this one), so its collection continues to grow. The Long Room is aptly named, and is in fact 200ft (64m) in length. Marble busts of Ireland's most famous scholars and literary men stand in serried ranks beneath the bookcases.

**6** At the east end of the Old Library building, the Treasury uses the latest in museum science to preserve some of the world's most valuable ancient manuscripts in pristine condition.

Christianity came to 'Holy Ireland' from Rome during the Dark Ages. An Irish princeling turned missionary, St Columba, brought Christianity from Ireland to Scotland, from where it reached the Angles of Northumbria and eventually the rest of Britain. Columba set up his first monastery on the Scottish island of Iona, which remained the spiritual home of Christianity in Scotland until repeated Viking raids forced the monks to abandon the island in the early 9th century AD, bringing their religious treasures with them. The Book of Kells, the gloriously, intricately illuminated manuscript which is the library's most precious treasure, is one of these. Brought by monks from Iona to the monastery of Kells, near Newgrange, it is the highest expression of a uniquely Celtic form of religious art. The Treasury also houses a portfolio of other superb illuminated manuscripts that are almost equally impressive and worth a look.

**TRINITY COLLEGE;**
www.tcd.ie

**7** Exit the Old Library, turn left and walk to the corner of the Old Library building at the northeast corner of Fellows' Square. Turn right briefly to bypass a small sunken garden, then left around the corner of the Berkeley Library Building. On your left is the

sward of New Square, the largest of Trinity's quadrangle lawns, and straight ahead of here you will see the Museum Building. This structure is a little at odds with the other buildings of the Trinity College Campus, but nevertheless an architectural triumph.

The Venetian façade of this Victorian building was designed by Benjamin Woodward and Sir Thomas Dean in 1857. Inside, the polychrome main hall and double-domed roof are more impressive than the slightly fusty collection of antiquarian exhibits, but the two towering skeletons of the giant red deer that once roamed Ireland's forests are worth a look.

**8** Turn about and walk back across the cobbled space between the Museum Building and the much more modern Berkeley Library, designed in 1967 by Paul Koralek.

Equidistant between the library and the museum is a huge, gleaming steel spheroid sculpture. This is *Sphere within a Sphere* (1982) by Arnaldo Pomodoro, which was a gift from the sculptor to Trinity. The Berkeley Library is named after another Trinity alumnus, the theologian Bishop Berkeley (1685–1753), who was famously vexed by the question of whether an event – such as a tree falling in the forest – could truly be said to have occurred if there was no one to observe it. He eventually concluded that since God is omnipresent and all-seeing, everything exists because he continually observes it.

**9** Turn left and walk along the east side of Fellows' Square, with the Berkeley Library on your left, then walk past the modern Douglas Hyde Gallery on your right to the Nassau Street exit from the campus. Turn right on Nassau Street to return to College Green.

ABOVE: *SPHERE WITHIN A SPHERE*, TRINITY COLLEGE

THE LONG ROOM OF THE OLD LIBRARY, TRINITY COLLEGE

# Around Parnell Square

**Parnell Square exudes a faded grandeur and is laden with memories of literary figures and victims of the fight for Irish independence.**

Parnell Square is long overdue for a facelift. This was once one of Dublin's grandest squares but, unlike Georgian and Victorian spaces on the south side of the city, it is a bit shabby and has been marred by insensitive modern buildings. That said, it still repays a visit with an array of hidden nooks and corners, historic buildings and insights into the lives of some of Dublin's most famous authors and playwrights. The square itself is named after one of the great tragic heroes of Ireland's 19th-century campaigns for self-government, and there are other mementoes of the independence struggle along the way. This walk can be easily combined with Walk 1.

**1** From the north end of O'Connell Street, cross Parnell Street and turn left. The green copper dome that gives the Rotunda Hospital its name is on your right, on the corner of Parnell Square East and Parnell Street. The entrance is on your right, set a little way back from Parnell Street behind a row of trees and shrubs.

Dublin dads-to-be still pop out of this grand 18th-century hospital to pace up and down the pavement and grab a quick smoke. Founded in 1745, the Rotunda is the first purpose-built maternity hospital in the world. The architect was German-born Richard Cassells (1690–1751; he later anglicized his name to Castle), who also designed Leinster House, seat of the Irish Parliament (see Walk 🥾), but the rotunda at the east end of the hospital, after which the building is now named, is an afterthought. Added in 1764, it was designed by John Ensor as a venue for concerts and events to raise money for the hospital and other charitable causes. Franz Liszt performed here in 1864. The hospital's most striking feature is its lovely chapel. Designed by Castle, its ornate interior is a feast of elaborate stucco, fluted pilasters and superb stained glass.

**2** With the hospital on your right, continue along the north side of Parnell Street to the end of the block and turn right on to Parnell Square West. The west front of the hospital is on your right. Walk past it to the end of the block, cross to the north side of Parnell Square North, turn right, then midway

## WHERE TO EAT

🍽 CONWAYS,
70 Parnell Street;
Tel: 873 2474.
This is a traditional pub, built in 1745, but the menu is much more modern and sophisticated than the 18th-century surroundings suggest. €

🍽 CHAPTER ONE,
Dublin Writers Museum,
18 Parnell Square;
Tel: 873 2266.
Portraits of famed authors gaze down on you as you enjoy the Italian-influenced menu here. €€€

along this short block turn left into Charlemont House, home of Dublin City Gallery The Hugh Lane.

Sir Hugh Lane amassed a remarkable collection of paintings by 19th-century Impressionists, including Manet and Degas, which in 1905 he offered to donate to the city on his death. The city corporation was unable to offer a suitable gallery in which to hang them, and only agreed to provide this elegant building after Lane threatened to give his collection to the National Gallery in London. Built in the mid-18th century, the building was originally the city home of Lord Charlemont. Sir Hugh Lane drowned in 1915 aboard the transatlantic liner *Lusitania* when it was torpedoed by a German U-boat, and Dublin and London squabbled for the next 50 years

23

DISTANCE  I mile (1.6km)

ALLOW  2–3 hours

START  Intersection of O'Connell Street and Parnell Street

FINISH  James Joyce Cultural Centre, North Great George's Street

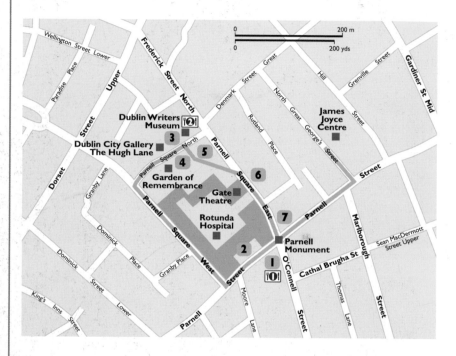

over which had title to the paintings. As a compromise, the collection now alternates between the two cities every five years. The gallery also has an excellent sculpture collection and a fine portfolio of work by contemporary Irish painters.

**THE HUGH LANE;**

www.hughlane.ie

**3** Continue along Parnell Square North to No. 18, an 18th-century townhouse that now houses the Dublin Writers Museum.

This museum lags slightly behind the times. It gives pride of place to Irish writers and poets from the dawn of Irish literature almost 1,000 years ago up to the early 20th century and the post-Independence period, but seems to have a bit of a blind spot when it comes to more recent contributors to Irish writing. The collection embraces manuscripts, first editions and letters, and for those who are interested in what their literary heroes looked like there is a fine portrait gallery upstairs. The museum bookshop offers a

specialist search service for rare and out-of-print editions of Irish authors.
**DUBLIN WRITERS MUSEUM;**

www.writersmuseum.com

**4** Cross to the south side of the street and enter the Garden of Remembrance at the north end of Parnell Square.

This little park is laden with memories of Irish freedom fighters. After the surrender of the Irish Volunteers holding the General Post Office in 1916, their leaders were held overnight here before being imprisoned in Kilmainham Gaol, where several were later summarily executed for their part in the Easter Rising. The garden was redesigned and dedicated as a memorial in 1966 on the 50th anniversary of the rising by President Eamon de Valera, himself a veteran of the war of independence. The pool in the centre of the garden is decorated with a mosaic of broken weapons, symbolizing an end to war, and the striking bronze statue beside it portrays the children of King Lir who, according to Irish myth, were turned into swans by a jealous stepmother. Oisin Kelly sculpted *Children of Lir* in 1971.

**5** Walk across the lawns of the square to the southeast corner, towards the rear of the Rotunda Hospital. You will see the Gate Theatre standing between you and the dome of the Rotunda at 1 Cavendish Row.

This grand theatre is another of Richard Castle's designs. Built in 1786 as the city's

Assembly Rooms, it was converted into a theatre some years after Independence, in 1928 with the intention of bringing new work by international playwrights to the Dublin public. More than 80 years on, the Gate is still recognized as Dublin's premier venue for new and classical drama.
**GATE THEATRE;**

www.gate-theatre.ie

**6** From the theatre, go down the left side of Parnell Square East for half a block, to the intersection of Parnell Square East, O'Connell Street and Parnell Street. In the centre of this intersection is the marble Parnell Monument, commemorating the 'uncrowned King of Ireland', Charles Stuart Parnell.

Like his forerunner Daniel O'Connell, Parnell sought to achieve self-government for Ireland through the existing political process. A Protestant by faith, he was elected to Parliament in London where he became a force to be reckoned with. Parnell built a strong movement for land reform and home rule, but his political alliance with the Liberal government of William Gladstone suffered as a result of the murder of Lord Frederick Cavendish, the British Chief Secretary for Ireland, by the extremist 'Invincibles', in Phoenix Park (see Walk 1). His credibility was destroyed when his affair with married woman Katharine O'Shea was exposed in 1890.

**7** Turn left, stay on the left-hand side of Parnell Street, and walk one short block to North Great George's

Street. Cross this, turn left, and less than halfway up the block turn right into the James Joyce Cultural Centre.

Although Joyce drew on his native city for the background and inspiration of all his towering works of literature, he quit Dublin as soon as he could at the age of 22 and came back only for a few brief visits. The Roman Catholic Church ensured that his books were classed as blasphemous and obscene and banned them in his native land. Those days are over, and Joyce is celebrated within this grand townhouse, which was originally built in 1784 for the Earl of Kenmare.

The author's characters – many of them thinly disguised pen-portraits of actual Dubliners – are also celebrated in the centre's key exhibit, a series of biographies of the real people on whom the characters in *Ulysses* were based. One of them, the fancifully named 'Professor Dennis J Maginni', held dancing lessons for ladies and gentlemen in this very house. It is said he awarded himself the title of 'professor', and that he Italianized his name to Maginni from the more mundane McGuinness to add a touch of Latin flair to his dancing academy.

**JAMES JOYCE CULTURAL CENTRE;**
www.jamesjoyce.ie

# The Green Heart of South Dublin

**St Stephen's Green is one of Dublin's best-loved public green spaces and a favourite spot for a lunch break or picnic on a summer day.**

The landscaped 22-acre (9ha) green is surrounded by gracious 18th-century buildings, and the green itself has a scattering of busts, memorials and monuments commemorating famous Dubliners. Until the 17th century the green was common grazing land, used for pasturing sheep and cattle on the outskirts of the city, but in 1664, in a land-grab typical of the times, it was arbitrarily 'enclosed' in an early and unpopular act of privatization. In 1880, in a belated act of generosity, its owner returned it to the city and the land was laid out as a formal garden with shrubberies, a lake and a bandstand that is still a venue for free concerts on summer afternoons. Depending on how much time you want to spend gazing at the prehistoric and medieval treasures in the National Museum, this walk can take as little as one hour or as long as half a day. For a longer walk, you can link it with Walk 2.

From the corner of Earlsfort Terrace, turn on to the south pavement of St Stephen's Green South. Almost immediately on your left, after less than 30 yards (27m), is Iveagh House, at 80 and 81 St Stephen's Green.

Richard Castle, the German-born architect who was responsible for so many of Dublin's grand 18th-century public buildings, designed No. 80 in the 1730s; his original façade was obliterated around 130 years later when this townhouse and the one next to it were knocked into one by Sir Benjamin Guinness. He commissioned a single front of Portland stone with the Guinness family crest above the front door. Guinness and his successors also carved out a pompous interior and bodged on a grand domed ballroom at the rear. The birth of the Irish Republic spelt the death of the gilded lifestyle of the Irish aristocracy, and in 1939 the 2nd Earl of Iveagh, Rupert Guinness, donated the building to the nation. It is now owned by the Foreign Department, and is used to host exclusive receptions for visiting bigwigs.

2 Carry on along the south side of St Stephen's Green South to Nos. 85 and 86, on your left.

If you are here in summer and have booked a guided tour, turn left into the most beautifully restored example of a grand Georgian interior with magnificent stuccowork, marble floors and elegant wooden staircases. Like

## WHERE TO EAT

[O] CITRON CAFÉ,
Fitzwilliam Hotel,
St Stephen's Green;
Tel: 478 7000.
Citron is a bright, trendy place to eat in one of Dublin's more fashionable hotels. The menu is imaginative and modern – try the smoked haddock risotto with baby spinach. €€

[O] THE HORSESHOE BAR,
Shelbourne Hotel,
27 St Stephen's Green;
Tel: 663 4500.
The grand bar of the Shelbourne Hotel is a St Stephen's Green landmark. It claims to be the most famous bar in Dublin and serves snacks and light meals as well as drinks. €€

[O] LA MERE ZOU,
22 St Stephen's Green;
Tel: 661 6669.
La Mere Zou offers excellent, traditional French cooking and fine local seafood. For a leisurely lunch or dinner rather than a quick snack. €€

its near neighbour, Iveagh House, it comprises two houses in one. The smaller of the two, No. 85, is largely the work of the ubiquitous Richard Castle. The house is named after John Henry Newman (later Cardinal Newman), who founded the Catholic University of Ireland here to provide an education for students

DISTANCE 1 mile (1.6km)

ALLOW 1–3 hours

START Corner of Earlsfort Terrace and St Stephen's Green South

FINISH National Museum of Ireland

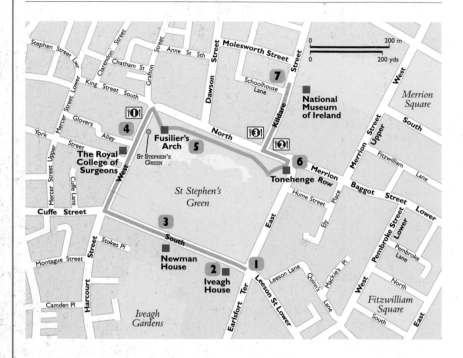

excluded from nearby Trinity because of their faith. Famous alumni include the authors James Joyce and Flann O'Brien (real name Brian O'Nolan) and the IRA leader and former president of Ireland, Eamon de Valera. The poet Gerard Manley Hopkins taught here, and his study is open to the public.

**NEWMAN HOUSE;**

www.ucd.ie/jhnewman

**3** Carry on along the south pavement of St Stephen's Green South. At the end of the block, turn right to cross the street, then cross St Stephen's Green West and walk up the west side of the park. The Royal College of Surgeons is midway up on your left, and dominates this side of the Green.

St Stephen's Green West is the least prepossessing aspect of the park, and the massive seven-bayed front of the college, built in 1810 and added to in 1825, is graceless by comparison with the earlier Georgian buildings nearby. Topping its

portico are three statues. From left to right as you face the building, these represent Hygieia, Greek goddess of health, Aesculapius, god of healing (whose symbol, a serpent twining around a stick, is sometimes still used outside hospitals and clinics) and Athena, goddess of wisdom. Like the General Post Office on O'Connell Street, the college still proudly bears the scars of the Easter Rising of 1916, when it was garrisoned by a contingent of the Irish Citizen Army led by Michael Mallin and the redoubtable Countess Constance Markievicz. Their detachment was the last to submit to the British, who later executed Mallin but reprieved Countess Markievicz. Hanging a woman, and an aristocrat at that, was apparently unthinkable, and she later went on to become the first woman to be elected to the British House of Commons.

**4** Pass by the college on your left, walk to the north end of St Stephen's Green West, recross the street and enter the park of St Stephen's Green by the entrance at its north corner, passing beneath Fusiliers Arch.

The arch was built in 1907 in honour of the Royal Irish Fusilier's, a regiment that served the British Empire well in many of its wars.

**5** From here, continue along Beaux' Walk, the path that runs along the north side of the park, with the lake on your right hand side, to the east corner of the park and the exit to Merrion Row. The Green's most prominent monument is in front of you.

Nicknamed 'Tonehenge' by irreverent Dubliners, this is sculptor Edward Delaney's memorial to Wolfe Tone (1763–98), leader of the United Irishmen in the abortive revolt of 1798. Like Charles Stuart Parnell, Tone was a Protestant as well as a committed Irish nationalist. His rising failed when France did not send enough arms, troops and ammunition to support his little army, and his supporters melted away. To this

day, he is still honoured as one of the founders of modern Irish nationalism.

**6** Leave the Green by its east exit, at the corner of St Stephen's Green North and St Stephen's Green East. Cross to the opposite side of St Stephen's Green East, turn left and after a few paces take the first right into Kildare Street. Stay on the right-hand side. The dignified Victorian buildings of the National Museum of Ireland are one third of the way up the block. Turn right to enter the museum courtyard through a pair of arched wrought-iron gates.

The National Museum's archaeology collection spans more than 9,000 years of Irish history and prehistory, but its newest section is the eerily fascinating 'Kingship and Sacrifice'. The peat bogs that still cover much of Ireland have weird preservative properties, and archaeologists have recovered the leathery cadavers of Iron Age men and women, along with tools, weapons and clothing. Some appear to have been strangled, suggesting that human sacrifice may have been practised in Ireland 3,000 years ago. Archaeologists speculate that in times of poor harvests a king or chief might voluntarily have been sacrificed as a way of sending a messenger to appeal to the gods for help. You could easily spend half a day here, marvelling at the intricate gold and bronze relics of the ancient Celtic world. The superb creations of the fusion of Irish and Norse cultures from the 9th to the 11th centuries are reminders that the Vikings were not entirely the coarse barbarians

that Christian chroniclers made them out to be. If time is limited, the essentials are the famous Tara Brooch, the Ardagh Chalice – a magnificent early Christian artefact – and the gorgeous prehistoric treasures collected in the 'Or – Ireland's Gold' section.

**NATIONAL MUSEUM OF IRELAND;**
www.museum.ie

**7** Buses 7, 7A or 8 from the opposite side of Kildare Street takes you back to Burgh Quay. Buses 10, 11 or 13 returns you to O'Connell Street. Alternatively, to link this with Walk 2, turn right out of the museum, walk past the National Library on your right, and at the end of Kildare Street cross Nassau Street and turn left. Take the first right into College Street to the entrance of Trinity College.

33

HA'PENNY BRIDGE ARCHING ACROSS THE RIVER LIFFEY

# Dublin's Cultural Quarter, Temple Bar

**Temple Bar's story is a tale of riches to rags and back to riches again, spanning some four centuries. This walk highlights the ups and downs.**

In the early 17th century, entrepreneur Sir William Temple acquired this strip of land on the south bank of the Liffey, spotting an opportunity for development as the city of Dublin began to expand south of the river. In the following centuries, Temple Bar grew into a teeming riverside district of chandlers' stores, warehouses, small businesses, tradesmen's workshops and overcrowded working-class housing. By the early 20th century it was a notorious slum, and in the 1960s the whole lot was slated for demolition. However, plans to build a new city bus terminus and road interchange were first put on hold for lack of money, then finally abandoned. This turned out to be a blessing in disguise for Temple Bar and Dublin as a whole. During the years of 'planning blight', while the authorities dithered over what to do with the district, small shops and workshops were rented on short-term leases to artists, musicians and designers. Temple Bar started to acquire a reputation for edgy art and design, and since the 1990s it has mutated into a 'cultural quarter' that now hosts more than 50 cultural organizations.

I Start on the north side of the
River Liffey by the end of Ha'penny
Bridge. Opened in 1816, this steeply
arched footbridge has more than one
nickname. It was first named after the
Duke of Wellington, is officially known
as the Liffey Bridge, and is sometimes
called the metal bridge. But its best-
known soubriquet comes from the
halfpenny toll charged to cross it until
1919. At its south end, cross Crampton
Quay to enter 'Dublin's Cultural
Quarter' by Merchant's Arch.

The arched gateway dates from the 18th
century. Until the mid-19th century,
merchant ships sailed up the Liffey to
load and unload along the quays on
either side. Later, larger steamships had
to dock further downriver, which had
a impact on Temple Bar — it began to
decline as it lost trade.

2 Through the arch, a short cobbled
alley lined with rather humdrum
souvenir shops leads to Temple Bar, the
original main street that has lent its
name to the entire district. Follow this
to the end and turn right, along the
north side of Temple Bar. Across the
street, on your left, is Temple Bar Square.
Crown Alley, which forms the east side
of Temple Bar Square, is lined with
trendy cafés, colourful designer stores
and small galleries. Carry on along
Temple Bar for one short block, cross
over Fownes Street, and enter the
Temple Bar Gallery at 5–9 Temple Bar,
just past the intersection of Temple Bar
and Fownes Street.

## WHERE TO EAT

[O] GALLAGHER'S BOXTY HOUSE,
20–21 Temple Bar;
Tel: 677 2762.
Potato-based boxty is Dublin's
signature dish and Gallagher's serves
up a mouthwatering array of boxty
pancakes with savoury fillings and
sauces, plus steaks, seafood and
vegetarian options. €€

[O] THE OLIVER ST JOHN
GOGARTY,
18 Anglesea Street;
Tel: 671 1822.
The bar menu here is strong on
seafood – Galway Bay oysters, Dublin
Bay prawns and generous helpings of
mussels – and this pub also serves
big all-day breakfasts and a variety of
good solid Irish cooking. €€

[O] THE TEMPLE BAR PUB,
47/48 Temple Bar;
Tel: 672 5286.
This traditional pub first opened its
doors in 1840 and serves oysters and
Guinness, a big choice of sandwiches
and, for cold-weather walkers, an
array of Irish coffees. €

The Temple Bar Gallery and Studios is
emblematic of the way the district has
recreated itself in the years since Dublin
was nominated European City of Culture
in 1991. A former factory, it offers
workshop and studio space to an array
of talented resident painters, printmakers,

37

DISTANCE **1.75 miles (2.8km)**

ALLOW **2 hours**

START **North end of Ha'penny Bridge**

FINISH **South end of Grattan Bridge**

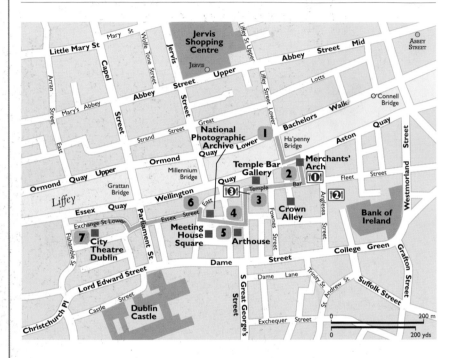

sculptors and other cutting-edge artists and has a rotating schedule of exciting exhibitions. Check the website before visiting to see what's on.

**TEMPLE BAR GALLERY;**

www.templebargallery.com

**3** Leaving the gallery turn right, take the first left on Temple Lane South and cross the street. Walk one block to Curved Street and go right. The Arthouse Multimedia Centre for the Arts is on the left, opposite Temple Bar Music Centre.

The Arthouse is a love-it-or-hate-it proposition. Curved Street is Dublin's newest street, and the Arthouse, like other buildings along this 21st-century crescent, is self-consciously modern, as are its contents and tenants. Traditionalists may cringe at its commitment to multimedia-based art projects, while technophiles will be excited at the touring exhibitions of video art and other cutting edge stuff. At the very least, the Arthouse's mission to bring technology and art together creates and fosters challenging work.

OPPOSITE: TEMPLE BAR MUSIC CENTRE

**4** Continue along Curved Street to its west end and then cross Eustace Street over to the east side of Meeting House Square.

This square, named after a Quaker meeting house that formerly stood here, has become the bustling hub of the cultural quarter. Meeting House Square is used in summer for midday and evening concerts of classical music, outdoor film screenings (tickets are free from the Temple Bar Information Centre, bring an umbrella) and more impromptu performances by passing street entertainers. A Saturday farmers' market sells a variety of produce ranging from Japanese sushi to Mexican burritos. Local organic items include breads, jams, yogurts and vegetables.

**5** Walk diagonally across to the north side of the square. The entrance to the National Photographic Archive is now facing you.

The National Photographic Archive (NPA) is an annex of the National Library of Ireland and has been housed here since 1998. Its three floors of exhibitions can show only a small percentage of its huge collection of around 300,000 images spanning more than 150 years and allowing you a fascinating glimpse of Dublin and Ireland in the vanished but not-so-distant past, when horse-drawn transport and steam power were the norm and people in the remoter parts of the country still warmed their homes with turf fires and dressed in age-old traditional costumes. The exhibits are rotated every three months, and there are also special thematic exhibitions; see the NPA website for details of what's on when to visit.

**NATIONAL PHOTOGRAPHIC ARCHIVE;** www.nli.ie

**6** After leaving the National Photographic Archive, turn right, then almost immediately turn right again to leave Meeting House Square from its northwest corner. Turn left on Temple Bar, cross the north end of Sycamore Street, and continue along the south side of Essex Street East for three

blocks, crossing narrow Crampton Court, Crane Lane and the wider Parliament Street to your left. After crossing Parliament Street, Essex Street merges into Essex Gate. Cross to the north side of Essex Gate, turn left, and at the next corner cross the foot of Exchange Street Lower and turn right up the west side of this street.

Dublin's City Theatre was founded in 1985 and moved into its new home in this striking space in September 2007. Now somewhat cumbersomely called City Theatre Dublin at the Empty Space, Smock Alley, this is a wonderful fusion of a historic site (the exterior of the building forms part of Dublin's medieval city walls) with a stunning interior designed by Jean-Guy Lecat. The original Smock Alley Theatre was one of the oldest in the world; built in 1662, it has been extensively restored and is now a rehearsal and performance venue for numerous Irish theatrical groups.

**CITY THEATRE DUBLIN;**

www.theatreireland.com

7 Leaving the theatre, backtrack to Parliament Street, turn left and walk down to Grattan Bridge, from where you can return to the city centre.

TRADITIONAL MUSIC, A FEATURE OF TEMPLE BAR PUBS

# Around Dublin Castle and Christ Church

**This part of the city has suffered from some not-too-sensitive modern building, but its ancient stones must be a highlight of any visit to Dublin.**

Just south of the Liffey lies the first heartland of Anglo-Irish Dublin, with the castle and Christ Church Cathedral as the kernels of a district studded with places of worship built under the Normans or in the heyday of the 'Protestant Ascendancy'; but before the Normans came earlier settlers and invaders. Prehistoric Celts dwelt near the mouth of the small River Poddle, which flowed into the Liffey close to where the castle now stands forming a natural harbour they called *Dubh Linn* – 'the Black Pool'. The charmingly named Poddle has long since been covered and built over, but as early as the 9th century the Liffey also attracted those inveterate river raiders and traders, the Vikings, who settled here around AD841. When the Normans came, they too saw the potential of this part of Dublin, and soon began work on the castle and a ring of defensive walls. Later still, as Dublin grew in size and importance, its rulers endowed the city with churches, cathedrals and religious foundations.

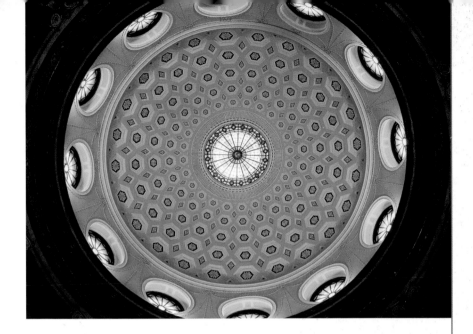

Cross the Liffey by Grattan Bridge, cross Wellington Quay on the south bank, and walk on down Parliament Street. The white pillars and copper-green rotunda dome of City Hall are right in front of you. Cross Cork Hill to enter.

Like so many of Dublin's grand public buildings, City Hall has served several masters. It was built between 1769 and 1779. Its architect was Thomas Pooley, whose design was better received than that proposed by the more famous James Gandon, architect of the Customs House and the Four Courts on the north side of the Liffey. It was originally intended to be Dublin's Royal Exchange, but in 1852 Dublin Corporation took it over, and it is still the seat of the city council. Mundane as that may sound, the vaults beneath now house 'The Story of the Capital', an exhibition that highlights the city's

history and is well worth a look. Look down as you enter the foyer below the rotunda at the mosaic floor, which bears Dublin's Latin motto: *'Obedientia civium urbis felicitas'* ('Happy the city where citizens obey') – an outstanding example of wishful thinking.

2 Leaving City Hall, turn left on Cork Hill and almost immediately left again to enter Dublin Castle.

The original seat of English power in Dublin is an architectural mish-mash, riddled with relics of imperial rule. Dublin's Anglo-Norman conquerors began building the castle in 1205, but virtually nothing remains of the original stronghold, though in the Undercroft you can see the scant remains of the Viking stronghold that preceded it. The castle grew under the Tudor and Stuart

43

OPPOSITE: DUBLIN CASTLE; ABOVE: CITY HALL DOME OF THE ROTUNDA

**DISTANCE** 1.6 miles (2km)

**ALLOW** 3 hours

**START** North end of Grattan Bridge

**FINISH** Corner of Parliament Street and Dame Street, outside City Hall

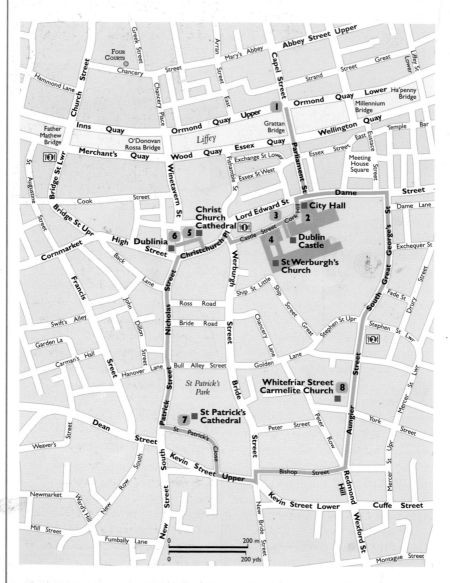

dynasties, but its present layout dates from the late 17th century. The complex was damaged by fire in 1684, after which is was redesigned and rebuilt. Until Irish independence, the castle was the residence of the British viceroy; thereafter, it passed into the hands of the Irish government, and the Lower Yard is used as government offices. The lavish State Apartments include the Throne Room, with a throne placed here by William of Orange (William III) in celebration of the victory of the Protestant cause at the Battle of the Boyne in 1690. Also within the State Apartments, St Patrick's Hall, once the banqueting hall of the defunct royal order of the Knights of St Patrick, has stunning 18th-century painted ceilings. The round, battlemented Record Tower is the oldest part of the building. It dates from 1258, but has been very extensively rebuilt and altered over the centuries. Next to it, the Church of the Most Holy Trinity, built in 1814, is the work of Francis Johnson, who along with James Gandon is probably the best-known contributor to Dublin's treasury of Georgian architecture. Look up as you leave by the Cork Hill entrance. Above the arch stands a statue of Justice, looking inward to the seat of English power and rather too symbolically turning her back on Dublin and Ireland.

**DUBLIN CASTLE;**

www.dublincastle.ie

3 Exit the castle, turn left into Castle Street, then after about 50 yards (45m) turn left at No. 7–8 to enter St Werburgh's Church.

St Werburgh's was begun in 1715 but remained unfinished until 1732. It was Dublin Castle's parish church until the building of Holy Trinity. Within the church are lavish memorials to members of the Guinness dynasty. In one of the vaults below lies Lord Edward Fitzgerald, one of the only aristocrats to join Wolfe Tone's unsuccessful rebellion in 1798. He was executed for his part.

4 Leave the churchyard, turn left and walk to the west end of Castle Street, and cross Werburgh Street to Christ Church Place. Cross to the north side and turn right to enter Dublin's oldest building, Christ Church Cathedral; the main entrance is through the west wing, to the left of the Romanesque doorway that opens on to the south transept.

ABOVE: CEILING PAINTING IN ST PATRICK'S HALL, DUBLIN CASTLE

Enter to be awed by the superb Gothic arches of the light and airy Great Nave. Richard de Clare decreed the building of Christ Church in 1172, on the site of a wooden church founded by Sidric, the Viking ruler of Dublin, in 1038. It was completed in 1240. De Clare's body is buried here, and the effigy of a recumbent, mail-clad knight known as the Strongbow Monument may have adorned his original resting place in the Great Nave. In the Chapel of St Laud, a heart-shaped phylactery chained to the wall holds the heart of Archbishop Laurence O'Toole, co-founder of the cathedral. Relics and monuments moved from the cathedral when it was rebuilt during the 1870s are in the crypt – among them the desiccated corpses of a cat and a rat that were discovered in one of the organ pipes.

**CHRIST CHURCH CATHEDRAL;**

www.cccdub.ie

5 Exit the cathedral by the graceful stone bridge facing the entrance and linking it with the Synod Hall.

This elegant neo-Gothic building, formerly the seat of the Synod of the Church of Ireland, now houses Dublinia and the Viking World, a twin exhibition that walks you back through medieval and pre-Norman Dublin. The best bit is the life-size reconstruction of a street from the Viking town that flourished on what is now Wood Quay.

**DUBLINIA AND THE VIKING WORLD;**

www.dublinia.ie

6 Recross the bridge to the cathedral, exit, cross to the south side of Christ Church Place. Turn round to place the cathedral on your right and turn left down Nicholas Street. Pass Ross Road, Bride Road and Bull Alley Street on your left. Immediately after Bull Alley Street is St Patrick's Park, and the cathedral is an obvious landmark. Walk to the foot of Patrick Street, turn left, and enter it.

Founded in 1191, Ireland's largest place of worship stands where St Patrick baptized his first converts to Christianity,

in AD450, at a sacred spring that was almost certainly a pre-Christian holy place. Author Jonathan Swift was dean here from 1713 to 1747, and Handel's *Messiah* had its first performance here under his auspices in 1742. Work on the great stone cathedral to replace Patrick's simple chapel began in 1192, on the orders of Archbishop John Comyn. It has been expanded and restored over the centuries, with the rebuilding of the 141ft (43m) Minot's Tower at the west end in 1370, the addition of the needle-pointed spire in the 18th century and restoration in the 19th century.

**ST PATRICK'S CATHEDRAL;**

www.stpatrickscathedral.ie

**7** Leave the cathedral and turn left down its south side along St Patrick's Close. At the end of the close, turn left onto Bishop Street Upper, cross Bride Street, and continue to the corner of Aungier Street. Turn left here, pass Peter Row on your left, then at 56 Aungier Street turn left into the churchyard of Whitefriar Street Carmelite Church.

Built in 1827, the church stands on the site of a 16th-century Carmelite priory. Its two big claims to fame are as the last resting place of St Valentine, whose relics, donated by Pope Gregory XVI in 1836, are buried beneath the saint's statue in the northeast corner, and as the home of an oak statue of the Virgin that dates from the 15th century, the only such religious effigy to have survived the flames of the Reformation and the destruction of Ireland's monasteries.

## WHERE TO EAT

**|O| BULL & CASTLE (FORMERLY CASTLE INN),**
5–7 Lord Edward Street;
Tel: 475 1122.
This homely, bustling gastropub serves steaks, grills and seafood and has a choice of 50 different beers as well as a good wine list. €€

**|O| GOVINDA'S,**
4 Aungier Street;
Tel: 475 0309.
The original Govinda's now has several siblings around Dublin, all serving a super array of Indian and Asian vegetarian dishes. An excellent lunch spot for veggies and non-veggies too. €€

**|O| THE BRAZEN HEAD,**
20 Bridge Street;
Tel: 677 9549.
www.brazenhead.com
Ireland's oldest pub opened its doors here in 1198. Good for a snack, a pint or a full meal, with bar menu and à la carte meals and the emphasis on hearty grub – oysters and Guinness, Irish stew, fish and chips and lighter dishes such as steamed mussels. €

**8** Retrace your steps to Aungier Street and follow it north to Great George's Street South. Carry on to the north end of Great George's Street South, turn left on Dame Street and walk the short stretch back to City Hall.

47

BEAUTIFUL ARE THE

OF THOSE THAT PREACH

GOSPEL OF PEACE

INSIDE ST PATRICK'S CATHEDRAL

# Along the North Bank of the Liffey

**A stroll along the north bank of the Liffey reveals grand buildings by an architect who endowed Dublin with many of its outstanding landmarks.**

Along the way this walk dips into the city's literary and artistic heritage, and passes reminders of some of the darker episodes in Dublin's history. The River Liffey is, in many ways, Dublin's reason for being. It attracted the first Celtic settlers, then the Vikings, and finally the Anglo-Norman invaders of the 12th century. The river cuts through Dublin from west to east, creating a city that, like London, has two identities, north and south of the river. And, of course, the water of the Liffey has for almost 300 years been the main ingredient of the drink that everyone associates with Dublin: Guinness, which is still brewed in vast quantities not far from the end of the walk (though Guinness have announced plans to relocate most of their operation to a site outside town).

I Start this walk on the south side of the Talbot Memorial Bridge, and look across and a little to your left to the remarkable façade of the Custom House.

This grand building with its verdigris copper dome, crowned by an allegorical statue of Commerce, is one of the triumphs of English architect James Gandon. Its history has not been happy. It became redundant only nine years after it was built, when Ireland's parliament was merged with Britain's and the customs and revenue offices moved to London. Through the 19th century it became more dilapidated, and in 1921 Sinn Fein firebrands administered the *coup de grâce*. The hated symbol of British rule burned for five days, and although it was patched up in the mid-1920s the building was not fully restored until 1991. Since then, it has housed various government departments.

2 Cross the bridge and turn left along Custom House Quay, passing the Famine Memorial on the left.

The potato has been both a blessing and a curse to Ireland. When it was introduced from America in the 17th century, it provided a cheap, plentiful and nourishing staple – so much so that by the 19th century many Irish families ate almost nothing else. When potato blight destroyed the entire crop, an estimated one million people starved to death. This was the Great Famine of 1845–48. Most of the deaths could have been prevented, but the British government was slow

to lift taxes and release stocks of grain (of which there was plenty) to feed the starving. Ireland's population fell by half over the next few decades, as millions of people emigrated to England, Scotland and America, and the number of people living in Ireland today is still well below the pre-famine level. Many of the people driven from their rural homes by hunger got no further than the Dublin slums, altering the character of the city forever.

3 Follow the north side of the quay, and take the next right after the Custom House, Beresford Place. Cross the street, pass Old Abbey Street on the left and take the next left into Abbey Street Lower. Ireland's national theatre is on the left side of the street at No. 26.

Ireland's 20th-century cultural renaissance began with the founding of the Abbey Theatre in 1904, by William Butler

51

DISTANCE **2.5 miles (4km)**

ALLOW **1 hour 30 minutes**

START **South side of the Talbot Memorial Bridge**

FINISH **Four Courts**

Yeats, Ireland's most famous poet, and his amanuensis, Lady Augusta Gregory. Many of the works first performed here – by playwrights including J. M. Synge, Sean O'Casey, Oscar Wilde, and more recently Brian Friel and Hugh Leonard – have been controversial and polemical, and the Abbey continues to be regarded as a theatre of global distinction. Its downstairs performance space, the Peacock Theatre, is dedicated to new talent.

**ABBEY THEATRE;**
www.abbeytheatre.ie

**4** Turn left from Abbey Street Lower on to Marlborough Street, return to

the riverside and turn right on Eden Quay. Follow this across O'Connell Street, after which it merges into Bachelors Walk.

At the west end of Bachelors Walk, the metal arch of the Ha'penny Bridge carries foot traffic across the Liffey. When it was built, in 1816, it was first named after the Duke of Wellington, then at the height of his fame as the victor of Waterloo. Its nickname comes from the halfpenny toll, which was charged to cross it, and was much resented. Since 1919, however, crossing has been toll-free.

**5** Pass the bridge and carry on along Ormond Quay Lower. On your right is the glitzy and pretentiously named 'Quartier Bloom', also known as the 'Italian Quarter'.

Opened in 2005, this mall-style shopping-and-eating development is completely inauthentic (Dublin has never had an Italian quarter until it was invented here) but it does have has some excellent restaurants and cafés and is a welcome addition to the riverside.

**6** Continue along Ormond Quay Lower. Across the street is the Liffey's newest bridge, erected here to mark the beginning of the last millennium.

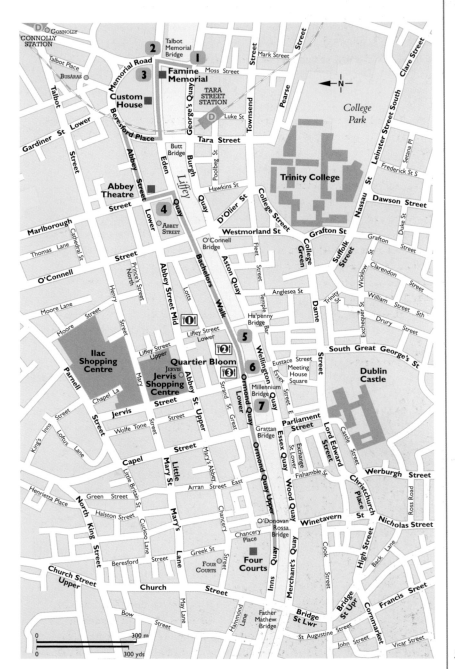

CONNOLLY
STATION

Talbot Place

BUSÁRAS

**2** Talbot
Memorial
Bridge

**1** Famine
Memorial

**3** Custom
House

Memorial Road

George's Quay

Moss Street

Mark Street

TARA
STREET
STATION

Luke St

Townsend

Pearse

Street

Clare Street

College
Park

←N→

Leinster Street South

Setana Pl

Frederick St S

Talbot

Street

Gardiner St Lower

Abbey Street

Beresford Place

Butt
Bridge

Eden

Tara Street

Burgh Quay

Liffey

Quay

Poolbeg St

Hawkins St

D'Olier St

Fleet

Street

College Street

Trinity College

Nassau

Dawson Street

Grafton St

Grafton

Street

Duke St

Abbey
Theatre

Marlborough

Street

Cathedral St

Thomas Lane

O'Connell

Prince's Street
North

Street

Street

Abbey Street Lower

**4**

ABBEY
STREET

Lotts

Bachelors Walk

Westmorland St

O'Connell
Bridge

Aston Quay

Anglesea St

College
Green

Temple Bar

Suffolk
Street

Wicklow

Clarendon

William

Exchequer St

Drury

Street

Street

Street

Moore Lane

Henry

Street

Moore

Liffey Street
Upper

Abbey Street Mid

Liffey Street
Lower

**5**

Ha'penny
Bridge

Dame

Trinity St

South Great George's St

Ilac
Shopping
Centre

Parnell

Street

Chapel La

JERVIS

Quartier Bloom

Jervis
Shopping
Centre

Abbey

Street

Wellington Quay

Essex

Street

Eustace Street

Meeting
House
Square

Essex St E

**6**

Street

Dublin
Castle

Jervis

Wolfe Tone Street

Street

Strand St Great

Ormond Quay Lower

Millennium
Bridge

**7**

Parliament
Street

Lord Edward

Street

Castle Street

Werburgh Street

Capel

Street

Little
Mary St

Mary's

Mary's Abbey

Arran Street East

Chancery

Ormond Quay Upper

Grattan
Bridge

Essex Quay

Exchange St Lower

Fishamble St

Wood Quay

Christchurch
Place

Ross Road

Nicholas Street

North King Street

Green Street

Little Britain St

Cuckoo Lane

Lane

Street

O'Donovan
Rossa
Bridge

Winetavern

Cook

High Street

Back Lane

Henrietta Place

Halston Street

Chancery
Place

Street

Street

Greek St

FOUR
COURTS

Four
Courts

Merchant's Quay

Inns Quay

Francis Street

Cormarket

Church Street
Upper

Beresford

Street

King's Inns St

Loftus Lane

Church

Street

May Lane

Bow

Street

Hammond
Lane

Father
Mathew
Bridge

Bridge
St Lwr

Bridge
St Upr

St Augustine Street

John Street

Vicar Street

0 ——— 300 m
0 ——— 300 yds

53

The pedestrian bridge was built in kit form in County Carlow, 50 miles (80km) from Dublin, then reassembled on the Liffey. The steel from which it is constructed came from Harland and Wolff, the Belfast shipyard that built the ill-fated *Titanic*.

**7** Continue along the riverside, crossing Capel Street (with Grattan Bridge on your left), Arran Street East and Chancery Place on your left, to Inns Quay. Ahead of you, overlooking the river, is a majestic building of pale grey stone capped by a green copper lantern dome supported by Corinthian columns.

The Four Courts building, completed in 1802, is James Gandon's finest work. Like Gandon's Custom House, where we began this walk, it fell victim to the violence of Ireland's independence struggle. In 1922, at the outbreak of the Irish Civil War, it was occupied by Republican fighters. In a grimly ironic re-enactment of the events of Easter 1916, the Free State army, commanded by Michael Collins, borrowed artillery and gunners from the British and shelled the Four Courts to rubble. As the building burned, the Republican leader Cathal Bruha charged out, still shooting, and was gunned down by Free State

THE FOUR COURTS, A LANDMARK ON THE NORTH SIDE OF THE LIFFEY

soldiers. The Civil War was a tragic, and ultimately pointless conflict between the faction of the independence movement, which accepted the Anglo-Irish Treaty of 1921, and the Republican faction, which repudiated it. The treaty created the Irish Free State, composed of the 26 counties that make up modern Ireland, but left the six counties of Ulster, where Protestants loyal to Britain were in the majority, under British rule. Collins, and other members of the Free State government, accepted it as the best deal they were going to get. Eamon de Valera, Brugha and other hardliners wanted nothing less than a fully independent Irish republic

## WHERE TO EAT

[O] PHOENIX BISTRO,
Millennium Walkway,
Abbey Street Middle;
Tel: 872 7295.
Smashing modern bistro with something for everyone, from bangers and mash to pizza, burgers, ciabatta, panini, wraps and salads. €€

[O] BAR ITALIA,
26 Ormond Quay Lower;
Tel: 874 1000.
Trattoria-style Italian restaurant with an excellent choice of pizzas, pasta and, for a faster meal, panini. €€

[O] CAFÉ CAGLIOSTRO,
Bloom Lane;
Tel: 888 0860.
A good spot for coffee – espresso, latte, cappuccino or whatever you fancy – cakes, biscuits and snacks. €

comprising all 32 counties. The war was a low-key conflict by modern standards, with casualties on either side in hundreds rather than thousands, but it left long-lasting scars. Collins was killed in an ambush in 1923; in May that year, de Valera ordered a ceasefire and returned to conventional politics. Nine years later, he was elected Taoiseach (prime minister), and remained prominent in Irish politics almost continuously, first as prime minister, later as president, until his death in 1973.

55

# A stroll around Phoenix Park

**One of the largest city parks in Europe offers a perfect escape from the
hustle and bustle of downtown Dublin.**

Why *Phoenix* Park? The name has nothing to do with the fire-born immortal
bird of ancient legend, but has a much more prosaic provenance. It derives from
the Irish *fionn uisce*, meaning 'clear water', the name of one of the springs that
rises here. Phoenix Park is claimed to be the largest city park in Europe. It
comprises more than 1,750 acres (700ha) of lawns, lakes, woodland and
shrubberies, and is sprinkled with monuments and memorials. Like many grand
English parks, Phoenix Park is designed to be a little wild and unkempt, and is
home to a herd of semi-wild deer. Indeed, Phoenix Park originated as a royal
deer preserve, created by the Duke of Ormond for King Charles II in 1662. A
later landowner, Lord Chesterfield, had it landscaped and opened it as a public
green space in 1745. It quickly became a favourite escape from the grimy city
for toffs and hoi polloi alike. Phoenix Park is a great place to stretch your legs
and grab a breath of fresh air at any time of year, but is undeniably at its best in
summer. Be aware that it may be a risky place to walk after dark.

**1** Enter the park through Park Gate, at its eastern tip. Chesterfield Avenue runs diagonally through the park from this gate to Castleknock Gate on the west side. A footpath leads off to the right immediately after you enter the park. Follow this to the People's Garden.

Laid out by the landscape architect Decimus Burton in the 1830s, this is the only formally designed part of the park, with pretty flowerbeds, shrubberies and two small ponds within the area known as Bishop's Wood.

**2** Follow the path anticlockwise through the wooded area and around the ponds, then return to Chesterfield Avenue and turn right.

On your left as you walk up the avenue is a graceless 204ft (63m) high granite pillar. This is the Wellington Monument, designed in honour of the hero of Waterloo by Sir William Smirke in 1817 and built with funds raised by public subscription. Though born in Ireland, Wellington denied his Irishness: 'Had I been born in a stable, would that make me a horse?', he once asked. The monument was intended to be taller than it is, but the builders ran out of money before it reached its planned height. Perhaps the people of Ireland valued Wellington no more than he valued his Irish roots. Money was eventually scraped together to recommence work, and it was finally completed in 1861. The bas–reliefs around its plinth, depicting Wellington's triumphs, are cast from the bronze of

## WHERE TO EAT

**|O|** RYAN'S OF PARKGATE STREET,
28 Parkgate Street;
Tel: 677 6097.
This authentic Victorian pub has been serving visitors to Phoenix Park since 1896. Good for a pint, a snack or a full surf-and-seafood meal. €

**|O|** NANCY HAND'S RESTAURANT,
30–32 Parkgate Street;
Tel: 677 0149.
Three separate bar areas (one devoted to coffee and tea), a carvery and a restaurant with a menu that stretches from Asian-style wraps to steak, grills and fresh seafood. €€

**|O|** LE PARC BISTRO,
26 Parkgate Street;
Tel: 671 3717.
Good salads, pizzas, pasta and a range of mains including variations on beef, chicken, pork, lamb and salmon. €€

captured French guns, of which there was no shortage after Waterloo.

**3** Proceed along Chesterfield Avenue, across Wellington Road, and turn right on Zoo Road to enter Dublin Zoo.

Founded in 1830, the zoo earns its place in history as the second oldest zoo in Europe. It has come on a bit since its early days, when its only inmate was a single wild boar. The zoo takes pride

57

**DISTANCE** 3 miles (4.8km)

**ALLOW** 3–4 hours

**START** Park Gate, corner of Conyngham Road and Infirmary Road

**FINISH** Ashtown Gate, corner of Castleknock Road and Blackhorse Avenue

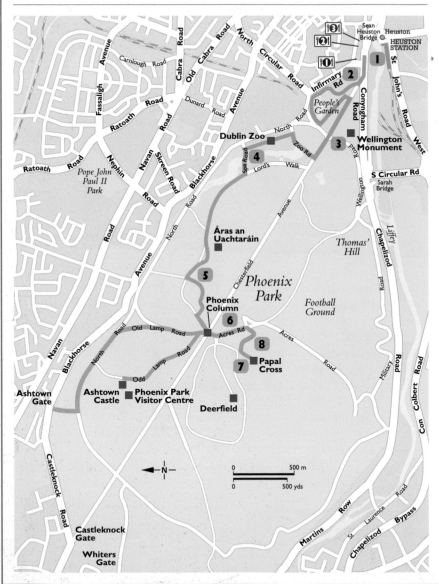

OPPOSITE: THE WELLINGTON MONUMENT

in its endangered species breeding programme – it began breeding lions as long ago as 1857, and film buffs will be interested to know that the original MGM lion was born here. Rhinos, giraffe and antelopes roam in the recently added African Plains section of the zoo.

**DUBLIN ZOO;**

www.dublinzoo.ie

**4** Leave the zoo by its north exit, on Spa Road, and turn left. At the corner of Spa Road and Lord's Walk, turn right on to the footpath that curves westward and you will see a rather grand white Palladian building ahead of you on your left.

Áras an Uachtaráin is the residence of the President of the Irish Republic. The building was designed by Nathaniel Clements in 1751, and was the country lodge of British viceroys until independence. It became the official home of Irish presidents in 1937. Eamon de Valera, president from 1959 until his death in 1973, served the longest term in residence.

**ÁRAS AN UACHTARÁIN;**

www.heritageireland.ie

**5** Follow the path as it curves southwest to the Phoenix Column, an unmissable landmark standing ahead and to your left.

This stone pillar, erected by Lord Chesterfield for the opening of the park in 1745, is said to mark the spot where the original spring that gave Phoenix

Park its name rises. Feeling witty, Chesterfield had the column crowned with a effigy of a phoenix, rising with outstretched wings from its own ashes. The phoenix is, of course, an entirely mythical creature, so the sculptor had to use his imagination. The result is not entirely convincing.

**6** Turn left (anticlockwise) at the Phoenix Column, then take the first left on Acres Road, almost doubling back on yourself. Follow Acres Road for about 300yards (275m) and take the first right. The road curves back westward to the Papal Cross, which will have been in sight all the way.

The 90ft (27m) steel crucifix marks the spot where Pope John Paul II held Mass before an audience of one million people when he visited Ireland in 1979.

**7** To the west of the Papal Cross, and partially concealed behind various security barriers, stands an elegant 18th-century mansion.

Deerfield was the home of Lord Cavendish, the British Chief Secretary for Ireland. Cavendish, with one of his aides, was assassinated in 1882 by nationalist extremists calling themselves 'the Invincibles', in what came to be known as the Phoenix Park Murders. The attack swayed public opinion in Britain against the Home Rule movement, and contributed to the political downfall of the Home Rule leader, Charles Stuart Parnell. This played into the hands of those nationalists who believed that Irish independence could never be achieved be peaceful means, and ultimately led to the tragedies of the Easter Rising and the Civil War. After independence, Deerfield passed into the hands of the Irish state, and is now the residence of the US Ambassador to Ireland. Famous guests have included John F. Kennedy, the first US President of Irish descent, who visited Dublin in 1963.

**8** Retrace your steps from the Papal Cross to the Phoenix Column. Walk clockwise round it, crossing Chesterfield Avenue, and turn left on to Odd Lamp Road. After just a few paces, turn left onto the footpath (signposted), which leads across the grass to Ashtown Castle ahead of you.

Built by an ancestor of Daniel O'Connell, this little tower house dates from a turbulent time. To make it easier to defend, there were no windows on the ground floor, and next to the door is a 'murder hole' through which a pistol could be fired at unwelcome visitors. Immediately to the west of the little castle is an attractive modern wooden building which houses the Phoenix Park Visitor Centre, with an interesting exhibition which follows the history of this patch of land from 3500BC to the 21st century. To leave the park, walk back to Odd Lamp Road and take North Road south to Ashtown Gate, from where you can catch buses back to the city centre.

**ASHTOWN CASTLE;**
www.heritageireland.ie

THE GROUNDS OF ASHTOWN CASTLE

# Georgian Dublin

**Dublin is in two minds about its Georgian golden age of architecture, and this walk explores some of the reasons why.**

Until the claims of the exiled House of Stuart to the thrones of Ireland, Scotland and England were finally quelled, and a German king of the House of Hanover sat firmly on all three thrones, Dublin remained what it had always been: an English outpost in a hostile land. But Hanoverian bayonets and turncoat politicians secured England's hold on its Irish and Scottish frontiers and Dublin became a piece of desirable real estate. From the early 18th century, anglicized Irish squires, aristocrats and compradors of the newly wealthy middle class began to show off their wealth by hiring architects and experts in plasterwork to build homes that displayed their prosperity. This was truly the heyday of what came to be known as the Protestant Ascendancy. Numerous architects contributed to the flowering of Georgian Dublin, but three – Richard Castle, James Gandon and Francis Johnson – stand head and shoulders above the crowd.

Fitzwilliam Square, a block east of St Stephen's Green, is a convenient place to begin the walk.

This small green space is surrounded on three sides by enviable 18th-century houses, most of which are now used as offices rather than private dwellings. Those that are private homes change hands for dizzying prices.

2 From the east side of the square, walk up Fitzwilliam Street and turn right into Baggot Street Lower.

With its terraced, elegantly proportioned houses of pale grey stone, Baggot Street is the epitome of Georgian Dublin. Typical of the period are the panelled doors, crowned by semi-circular fanlights and flanked by white-painted stucco pillars. Many retain their original polished brass doorknobs and knockers, and most are painted in bright colours that add a dash of whimsy to the staidly dignified elegance of this and other Georgian streets.

3 Cross over Baggot Street to the north side and walk up James's Street East for one block to Mount Street Upper. Turn left, stay on the left-hand side, walk one very short block and turn left to 29 Fitzwilliam Street, at the corner of Mount Street Upper and Fitzwilliam Street Lower.

No. 29 (the Georgian House Museum) offers a rare glimpse into the world of Georgian Dublin's well-off bourgeoisie, with an interior furnished and decorated as it would have been in the late 18th or early 19th century. Authentic in every detail, it houses period works of art, china and silverware, mirrors and paintings, as well as more mundane kitchen utensils and household equipment. Start in the basement and work your way through the living and dining rooms on the lower floors to the bedrooms, then the children's nursery in the attic, for the full tour.

**GEORGIAN HOUSE MUSEUM;**
www.esb.ie/no29

4 Turn right out of No. 29, cross Mount Street Upper and walk up the east side of Merrion Square, passing on the way a fine array of 18th-century townhouses. At the corner of the square, turn left on its north side and then left again to enter the square.

This is Dublin's most elegant Georgian square, landscaped around 1762 by James

65

**DISTANCE** 2 miles (3.2km)

**ALLOW** 1 hour

**START** Fitzwilliam Square

**FINISH** Newman House (St Stephen's Green South)

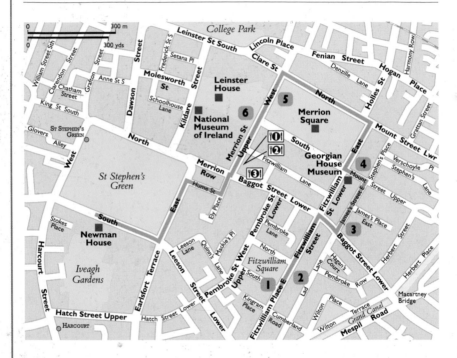

Ensor, which has had more than its share of famous residents, among them W. B. Yeats, whose Dublin home was No. 82, and Daniel O'Connell, who lived at No. 58. Walk along the north side of the square to the north corner, where a disturbingly lifelike, dandified figure reclines on a convenient boulder. This is, of course, Oscar Wilde, whose childhood home was at No.1 Merrion Square. Another famous resident was Arthur Wellesley, later Duke of Wellington, who was born at No. 24 Merrion Street

Upper, just south of the square. Midway down the west side of the square is a prominent drinking fountain, the Rutland Fountain, built into the railings. It was erected here in 1792 to provide a water supply for the poorer residents nearby. At that time the grand homes around the square had all the modern conveniences of the period (though their plumbing was pretty primitive by 21st-century standards) but working-class homes lacked any kind of indoor plumbing or water supply.

**5** Leave Merrion Square by the west side, cross the street and turn left. Leinster House, the home of Ireland's parliamentary chambers, the Dáil and the Seanad, occupies most of the block.

From Merrion Square West and Merrion Street Upper, you're looking at the rear of Leinster House, over gardens that give it the appearance of a grandee's country house. It was built for the Duke of Leinster, who commissioned the ever-busy German-born architect Richard Castle (originally Cassels; 1690–1751) to design it. The Fitzgerald dynasty, Earls of Kildare and Dukes of Leinster, were the grandest of Irish grandees, owning vast estates, intermarrying with Irish magnates and virtual rulers of their own territory. Thomas Fitzgerald, son

of the 9th Earl, joined the pantheon of Irish martyrs when his revolt against the English King Henry VIII failed in 1534. As an aristocrat, he was allowed to be hanged with a silk rope – hence his posthumous soubriquet, 'Silken Thomas'. His unfortunate followers were hanged with the usual rough hempen noose. By the time Leinster House was built, however, the Fitzgeralds – like most of the original Anglo-Norman dynasties – had reached an understanding with the ruling power. You may wonder how Castle found the time to plan so many of Dublin's great buildings – either he had a superhuman capacity for hard work, or (more likely) a team of hard-working and unsung assistants. Leinster House was completed in 1745, but 70 years later the Duke's descendants – who were by that

time more interested in cutting a dash in London than in being big fish in the shrinking pool of Dublin society – sold it to the Royal Dublin Society. In 1922 the Free State government acquired part of the building, and in 1924 it bought the entire building to house the new national government.

**6** With Leinster House on your right, walk down the right-hand side of Merrion Street Upper, past the National Museum of Ireland, to Baggot Street Lower. Cross this, walk a few steps down Ely Place, then turn into Hume Street. At the end of this short street, turn left on to St Stephen's Green East. At the foot of this street (opposite the southeast corner of St Stephen's Green) turn right and cross the street to the south side of St Stephen's Green South. Follow this to No. 85 and 86, on your left midway along the block.

Newman House is another outstanding example of the work of Richard Castle, the architect of Leinster House. The immaculately restored interior features Castle's trademark stuccowork, marble floors and elegant wooden staircases. The building (two houses conjoined) is named in honour of John Henry Newman (later Cardinal Newman), founder of the Catholic University of Ireland whose famous alumni include the authors James Joyce and Flann O'Brien (real name Brian O'Nolan) and Eamon de Valera. The poet Gerard Manley Hopkins, whose study is open to the public, was one of its professors. To return to the city centre on

## WHERE TO EAT

**[O] CELLAR BAR,**
Merrion Hotel,
Merrion Street Upper;
Tel: 603 0600.
www.merrionhotel.com
In the wine vaults, light meals include *charcuterie* platter, *foie gras*, salmon fishcakes and more. €€/€€€

**[2] PATRICK GUILBAUD,**
21 Merrion Street Upper;
Tel: 676 4192.
www.restaurantpatrickguilbaud.ie
The lunchtime set menu is surprisingly affordable, but the much costlier, nine-course gastronomic menu is an experience to savour. €€€

**[3] DOHENY & NESBITT,**
4–5 Baggot Street Lower;
Tel: 676 2945.
This magnificent old pub with its ornate ceiling, wooden floors, Victorian mirrors and long bar is a favourite with Dubliners. €

foot takes about 15 minutes (turn right at the end of St Stephen's Green South, walk up the west side of St Stephen's Green and then follow Grafton Street past Trinity College. Alternatively, return to the corner of Earlsfort Terrace and St Stephen's Green South, which is served by several buses.

**NEWMAN HOUSE;**
www.ucd.ie

# Museums and Galleries
# of South Dublin

**Exploring Dublin's museums plunges you back into the city's glittering past, giving a deeper understanding its fascinating heritage.**

More than 1,000 years of Irish history and culture are represented in Dublin's magnificent museums, along with antiquities and works of art gifted to the city by some of its wealthier residents. To make the most of the world-class collections of the National Gallery, the depths of the National Museum and the Dublin Civic Museum, not to mention the ancient tomes of the National Library and Marsh's Library, you should probably plan to make a full day of it. The distance covered by this walk is not great, but each of the stops along the way merits a pause of at least half an hour, and you could easily spend up to two hours in the National Gallery, and an hour or more in the National Museum. If your plans include tracking down your Irish ancestors, you should allow at least an hour in the Heraldic Museum's Genealogical Office.

Get off the bus on the north side of Merrion Square, about face, and walk to the corner of Merrion Square West. Cross the street, turn left and immediately to your right enter the National Gallery through a triple-columned 19th-century portico.

This is a world-class gallery, with more than 500 works of art in its collection. For a fast visit, turn left on entering, into the Shaw Room. The eminent playwright George Bernard Shaw (1856–1950) left much of his estate to the gallery, and this room is a showcase for portraits of the great and the good of Dublin and Ireland, from the Elizabethan period to the early 20th century. From the Shaw Room, carry on to the Yeats Museum, with its collection of portraits by John Butler Yeats and landscapes by his son Jack B. Yeats, (brother of the more famous W. B.). The central aisle of the ground floor comprises the Irish gallery. On the first floor, French, Spanish, Dutch, Flemish and German Renaissance painters are on show. Pride of place goes to Caravaggio's *The Taking of Christ*. Painted in 1602, this splendid painting vanished for several centuries until its rediscovery in Dublin's Jesuit House of Study in 1990.

**NATIONAL GALLERY OF IRELAND;**

www.nationalgallery.ie

**2** Leave the gallery, turn left, return to the corner, turn left again and walk three blocks – first along Clare Street, then, after passing Clare Lane on your left, along Leinster Street South – to the

## WHERE TO EAT

**⬛ TOWN BAR AND GRILL,**
21 Kildare Street;
Tel: 662 4800.
www.townbarandgrill.com
Modern Italian cuisine accompanied by an extensive list of Italian and New World wines. €€

**⬛ WAGAMAMA,**
King Street South;
Tel: 478 2152.
www.wagamama.ie
Trendy noodle restaurant serving modern Japanese dishes. €

**⬛ THE OLD STAND,**
37 Exchequer Street;
Tel: 677 7220.
www.theoldstandpub.com
Solid old-fashioned pub with a traditional menu of steaks, burgers, apple pie leavened with lighter offerings such as quiches, salads and wraps. €€

corner of Kildare Street. Immediately after you turn the corner, the Heraldic Museum and Genealogical Office is on your left. Its red-brick, faux-Venetian façade makes it conspicuous.

If your name is Timothy, Mick or Pat, or if you think there's even a hint of Irish in your ancestry, this is the place to come to track down your forebears. For around five centuries, Ireland has sent millions of its sons and daughters overseas, to

DISTANCE **2.5 miles (4km)**

ALLOW **All day**

START **Merrion Square North**

FINISH **St Patrick's Close**

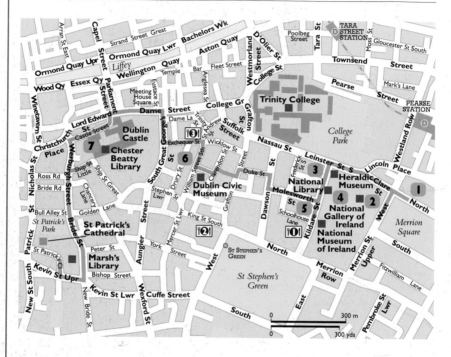

England, Scotland, mainland Europe, the Americas and Australia. The 'Wild Geese' – exiled Catholic aristocrats and their followers – fought in the armies of France and Spain against England in the 17th and 18th centuries. One descendant of an Irish émigré, Marichal Macmahon, went on to become a president of France; another Irish soldier of fortune, Bernardo O'Higgins, is celebrated to this day as the *Libertador* (Liberator) and first president of the Chilean Republic; Australia still has a soft spot for Ned Kelly, the greatest

bushranger of them all; and two US presidents in the second half of the 20th century share Irish bloodlines. So if you have a trace of Ireland in your DNA, you're in interesting and varied company. The Genealogical Office staff are available (for a small fee) to help you on your way down memory lane, but do as much homework as you can before you arrive. You can download a preparatory questionnaire from their website.

**GENEALOGICAL OFFICE;**

www.nli.ie

**3** Exit to Kildare Street, turn left, and walk only a few yards down the street to the entrance of the National Library of Ireland, next to the Heraldic Museum. Turn left to enter.

Founded in 1890, the library's exhibits include manuscripts by Irish literary greats including George Bernard Shaw and W. B. Yeats, photographs and a hand-written copy of one of the earliest written works about Ireland, Giraldus Cambrensis's *Topographia Hiberniae (Topography of Ireland)*, dating from the 13th century.

**NATIONAL LIBRARY OF IRELAND;**
www.nli.ie

**4** Back on Kildare Street, turn left and after a few steps enter the wrought-iron gates of the National Museum of Ireland – Archaeology and History.

This is the National Museum's archaeology collection. The archaeology collection spans more than 9,000 years of Ireland's history, and you should aim to spend at least an hour here. The most immediately impressive exhibits are the intricate gold and relics of the ancient Celtic world in the 'Or – Ireland's Gold' section, which is one of the largest collections of gold ornaments from prehistory anywhere in Europe. The craftsmanship of the amulets, collars, torcs and bracelets shown here is as fine as anything from the world of ancient Greece or the tombs of the Egyptian pharaohs. The finest individual exhibits include the famous gold and silver Tara

Brooch, set with amber and emeralds, and early medieval Christian artefacts such as the Ardagh Chalice and the 12th-century Cross of Cong. The museum's newest section is the creepy 'Kingship and Sacrifice' exhibition of mummified Iron Age bodies, along with tools, weapons and clothing, which have been discovered in Irish peat bogs.

**NATIONAL MUSEUM OF IRELAND;**
www.museum.ie

**5** Cross Kildare Street, turn right for a few yards, then take the first left into Molesworth Street. Follow this past Frederick Street on your right to Dawson Street. Cross the street, turn right, then almost immediately turn left into Duke Street, which leads to Grafton Street. Turn left then right, and walk two short blocks, crossing Clarendon Street, to the Dublin Civic Museum at the corner of William Street South.

There's a sense that the Civic Museum ended up with the exhibits that better endowed collections didn't want. Its oddballs include the huge slippers once owned by the tallest man ever born in Ireland, and the somewhat battered stone head of Nelson that crowned his pillar on O'Connell Street until it was demolished by an IRA bomb in 1966. (At the time of writing, the museum was closed awaiting details of relocation.)

**6** From the museum, turn right up William Street South to the corner of Exchequer Street. Turn left, pass Drury Street on your left, then turn right on Great George's Street. At the corner of Dame Street (not Dame Lane, which is on your right just before), turn left, pass the City Hall on your left, and turn left again to enter Dublin Castle via the Cork Hill entrance. The Chester Beatty Library and Oriental Collection are housed in the Bermingham Tower, at the southwest corner of the complex.

The millionaire American aesthete Alfred Chester Beatty left his amazing collection of European religious books and manuscripts, Middle Eastern Korans, Egyptian papyri, beautiful Chinese jade books and works of art and craftsmanship from Thailand, Burma and Japan, to the Irish people, earning him honorary Irish citizenship in 1957.

**CHESTER BEATTY LIBRARY;**

www.cbl.ie

**7** Leave the complex through the Ship Street Little entrance. Turn left on to Werburgh Street and continue to the corner of Bride Street and Kevin Street Upper. Turn right, then take the first right into St Patrick's Close and almost immediately after the corner turn right into Marsh's Library.

For scholars, this is a treasury of more than 25,000 antiquarian books and manuscripts. For dilettantes, the library built for Archbishop Narcissus Marsh by the architect Sir William Robinson in 1701 is a fascinating glimpse into the intellectual world of the 17th and 18th centuries. This, the oldest public library in Ireland, has remained unchanged since it was built, and its glowing wood panelling and elaborate fretwork are symbols of an earlier era of information technology, when the printed word still ruled. To return to the city centre, turn right out of the building and follow St Patrick's Close to Patrick Street. Buses to Eden Quay leave from the stop opposite.

**MARSH'S LIBRARY;**

www.marshlibrary.ie

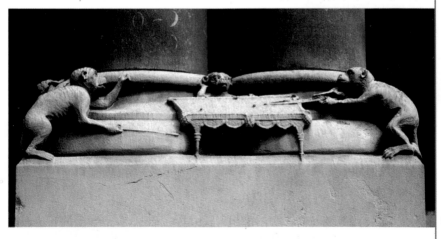

DETAIL AT THE FOOT OF A COLUMN, NATIONAL LIBRARY OF IRELAND

READING ROOM, NATIONAL LIBRARY OF IRELAND

# A Bloom's Day

**If a work of fiction can be said to be a paean to a city, it must be James Joyce's *Ulysses*, following a day in the life of Leopold Bloom in Dublin.**

James Joyce (1882–1941), arguably Dublin's finest writer, was already a successful author by the time he wrote his greatest work, *Ulysses,* in 1922. *Dubliners*, a collection of short stories about his native city, and *A Portrait of the Artist as a Young Man*, his semi-autobiographical novel, had already established him in Irish literary circles. But *Ulysses*, covering the wanderings of Jewish Dubliner Leopold Bloom on 16 June 1904, is an unmitigated masterpiece – funny, moving, thought-provoking, while weaving in classical themes influenced by parallel plot conventions of Homer's *Odyssey*; each chapter echoes a chapter in Homer's work and employs its own style. There are literally hundreds of Dublin locations mentioned in the novel, many of which are no longer in existence, but this walk takes in just a few that give a flavour of Bloom's own journey. If you happen to be in Dublin on 16 June, now known as Bloomsday, you will most likely be taking this popular route accompanied by crowds of fellow fans.

1 Begin by taking bus 40A from O'Connell Street to Dorset Street and when you disembark turn left into Eccles Street.

In *Ulysses,* Leopold and Molly Bloom lived at No. 7 Eccles Street. That house has since been knocked down, though the front door is preserved at the James Joyce Cultural Centre (see Walk 3). Opposite what would have been No. 7, however, is another typical Georgian style house (No. 78), which now has a plaque saying 'Bloom House' in honour of the novel. This is where a large crowd usually gathers at the starting point of the annual Bloomsday celebrations.

2 Walk back to the eastern end of Eccles Street and turn right on to Dorset Street. Continue straight down, taking the left fork at the bottom on to Capel Street, then the first right on to Little Britain Street.

In Chapter 12, Bloom stops for a drink in Barney Kiernan's pub and has various conversations with other customers, generally heated, about a number of topics, including capital punishment, nationalism, the nature of being Jewish, and even the wonders of Guinness. In the original concept of the book the chapter was called 'Cyclops' (Joyce later abandoned giving each chapter names relating to the *Odyssey,* feeling that it was a little over-stylized), which refers to the narrow-mindedness of the publican (Cyclops was the one-eyed monster in Homer's work).

3 Return to Capel Street, turn right and walk down to the abbey on your right on Meetinghouse Lane.

Chapter 10 of the novel, originally called 'Wandering Rocks', is a disjointed piece of snapshots of various characters around Dublin. Here, characters named Ned Lambert and J. J. O'Molloy (also one of the customers in discussion in Barney Kiernan's) meet the reverend of St Mary's Abbey and they discuss the history of the building. Founded in 1139 as a Benedictine monastery, only one room now remains, but it is a beautiful example of medieval architecture with a beamed vaulted ceiling.

4 Turn back on yourself and walk down Abbey Street Upper until it meets Abbey Street Middle.

**DISTANCE  3 miles (4.8km)**

**ALLOW  3 hours**

**START  Eccles Street**

**FINISH  Grafton Street**

The *Freeman* newspaper offices, which feature in Chapter 7, located in Abbey Street Middle, are in fact the offices of the building now occupied by the *Irish Independent* newspaper. Bloom's profession is advertising and he visits the newspaper offices to discuss the printing of a new advertisement for one of his clients. The literary style of the chapter reflects its subject matter, being broken up after every paragraph with a new 'headline'. The Oval pub, which stands a little further down the street, also features in this chapter.

5 Turn left on to O'Connell Street and walk north one block.

Joyce's description of the goings on at the General Post Office at the start of Chapter 7 are wonderfully evocative of the frenetic pace of the city's main postal depot as well as the transport hub that was O'Connell Street (and still is today). The unmistakable silver 'Spire' that now towers over O'Connell Street is a replacement for the Nelson Pillar mentioned in the novel, which was sadly destroyed by the IRA in the 1960s.

DAVY BYRNES PUB IN THE CENTRE OF DUBLIN

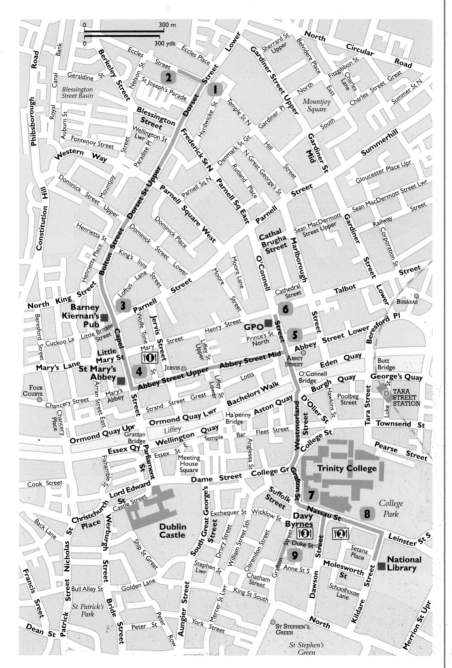

## WHERE TO EAT

**⌘ JOHN M. KEATING BAR,**
Mary Street at Jervis Street;
Tel: 828 0102.
Set in a converted church that still has original stained-glass windows and an organ, this bar makes an atmospheric refreshment stop. €€

**⌘ KILKENNY CAFÉ,**
5–6 Nassau Street;
Tel: 353 1 677 7075.
As well as a café and a more formal restaurant, this is also a shop selling traditional Irish crafts and foodstuffs. €

**⌘ DAVY BYRNES,**
21 Duke Street;
Tel: 677 5217.
Featured in the novel *Ulysses*, this pub has a wonderful 1930s interior and serves great Irish fare, such as oysters and Irish stew. €

**6** Walk back down O'Connell Street towards the river, over O'Connell Bridge, and take the right fork along Westmoreland Street to College Green.

Bloom walks past Trinity College in Chapter 8 on his way to Davy Byrnes and doesn't have many complimentary things to say about the 'surly front' of the building. This may well be because Joyce, unlike many of his contemporaries, did not study at Trinity but instead at University College Dublin.

**7** Continue down Grafton Street, turn left into Nassau Street and walk to the corner of Nassau and Kildare Street, home of the National Library.

Stephen Dedalus has a heated debate in the National Library about Shakespeare, generally analyzing the play *Hamlet* and the relevance of Shakespeare's wife Ann Hathaway to the playwright's work. Stephen, who features in Joyce's earlier works, is a poet who takes his literary aspirations very seriously. Bloom also appears at the library in search of a particular book.

**8** Return back up Nassau Street and turn left on to Dawson Street and then right on to Duke Street.

No. 21 Duke Street is Davy Byrnes pub, where Bloom has lunch in Chapter 8 and muses about the nature and variations of food. On Bloomsday the pub is extremely crowded with Joyce fans enjoying the same meal as Bloom – a cheese sandwich and a glass of red wine. Joyce himself was a regular at the pub, which also features in one of the stories in *Dubliners*.

**9** Walk to the end of Duke Street and turn left on to Grafton Street.

The opticians that Bloom window-shops at in Chapter 8, before lunching at Davy Byrnes, was Yeates & Son on Grafton Street, which is no longer there. The greengrocer Thornton's, mentioned at the start of Chapter 10, was also on Grafton Street.

OPPOSITE: NEWSPAPER OFFICES ON ABBEY STREET MIDDLE

# Dublin's Men of Letters

**Many cities boast a strong and extensive literary heritage but few celebrate their home-grown wordsmiths with such fervour as Dublin.**

From the solemnity of St Patrick's Cathedral, to the tranquillity of Dublin's garden squares, to the hotbed of Irish nationalist drama in the early 20th century, this walk not only explores the extraordinary influence of some of Ireland's greatest writers, but also takes in a large proportion of central Dublin along the way. It's a walk that should be undertaken at leisure: down small streets of Georgian houses, through landscaped gardens where locals picnic and sunbathe in summer, along the banks of the Grand Canal, past the hallowed halls of Trinity College and then over the Liffey, looking down on the river that is so intrinsic to Dublin's character. All the while you can ponder how these streets and buildings inspired works as diverse as *Gulliver's Travels*, *Pygmalion* and *Dracula*. It would be best to do the walk in the afternoon (Monday to Saturday) if you want to end with a performance at the Abbey Theatre in the evening, but be warned that for popular productions you will generally need to have booked tickets in advance.

> At St Patrick's Close, walk through the main entrance to the cathedral.

Given the lively celebrations that take place around the world on St Patrick's Day each year wherever there is a contingency of Irish descendants, it's fair to say that Ireland's patron saint is still a much revered figure in the country's history. Dublin's cathedral in his honour dates from 1191 and although it plays something of a second fiddle to the larger Christ Church Cathedral, it has been the focus of many important events, including the inaugural performance of Handel's great oratorio *The Messiah*. Its literary heritage, however, is linked to Jonathan Swift (1667–1745) who was dean of the cathedral from 1713 to 1745. Having studied at Trinity College, followed by a spell in England, he ordained to the priesthood in the Church of Ireland in 1694. His religious convictions, however, did not prevent him from expressing his strong political views, notably about the Tory government of the time, and he already had a reputation as both a satirist and a political campaigner before he penned his best-known work, *Gulliver's Travels,* in 1726. Telling the tale of the giant Gulliver who finds himself shipwrecked on Lilliput, a country of tiny people only 6in (15cm) tall, it is also a subtle allegory on politics and religion, as well as an examination of human nature. Just to the right of the cathedral's entrance is an area commemorating Swift and his association with the building, including the pulpit from which he preached, his death mask and his epitaph, the last line of which can be translated as 'he served human liberty'. In front of this area on the ground are the gravestones of both Swift and Esther Johnson, the woman he immortalized in his poetry as Stella.

**ST PATRICK'S CATHEDRAL**

www.stpatrickscathedral.ie

> With your back to the cathedral follow St Patrick's Close round and turn left on to Kevin Street Upper. Take the first right on to Bride Street, and follow this road straight down until it turns into Heytesbury Street. Turn left on to Grantham Street, then right on to Synge Street.

At No. 33 Synge Street is the birthplace of one of the most prolific playwrights of

85

**DISTANCE** 3.5 miles (5.5km)

**ALLOW** 3 hours

**START** St Patrick's Cathedral, St Patrick's Close

**FINISH** Abbey Theatre, Abbey Street Lower

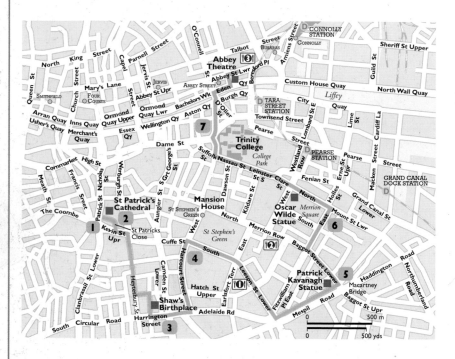

19th- and 20th-century literature, George Bernard Shaw (1856–1950). Although he spent the majority of his adult life in England, his Irish roots gave him much of the humour that is apparent in his plays as well as a strong conviction about social standards. Among his best-known plays are *Pygmalion* (probably better known today as the musical *My Fair Lady*), *Arms and the Man* and *Mrs Warren's Profession*, but in all his works he explored matters of social convention or injustice, from the class system, to education, to women's rights, to religion, yet managing to add comedic elements that prevent the works from being pure diatribes. A plaque outside his birthplace is rather less eloquent than the man, saying simply 'author of many plays', but inside, his first home has been turned into a museum in honour of the Nobel Prize winner. There are the inevitable displays detailing the life and works of Shaw but of rather more interest is the meticulous reconstruction of a house exactly as it would have been in Victorian times.

**3** Continue south down Synge Street and turn left on to Harrington Street, crossing over the junction with Camden Street. Turn left into Harcourt Street.

A plaque at No. 16 commemorates possibly the most famous horror writer in history, Bram Stoker (1847–1912). Although born in the Dublin suburb of Clontarf (where there is now a rather tacky museum entitled The Bram Stoker Experience), he attended Trinity College and lived at this address for a time before moving to and settling in London. Fascinated by folklore, which he drew upon in a number of horror novels, the work that has earned him a place in literary history and spawned a whole cinematic genre is *Dracula*, the tale of the infamous Transylvanian vampire count. With a chill in your step, move on to an altogether gentler man of letters.

**4** At the top of Harcourt Street turn right on to St Stephen's Green

South, then follow the right fork at the end of this street down Leeson Street Lower. As you get to the canal turn left on to Mespil Road.

Near the Macartney Bridge on the Grand Canal is a wonderfully reflective statue of the poet Patrick Kavanagh (1904–67) sitting on a park bench, whose works, such as *Stony Grey Soil* and *Canal Bank Walk,* explore the desire and need for a simpler life and a return to nature. Kavanagh used to come and sit by the canal after suffering from lung cancer and found its quietness and solitude a great inspiration to him, hence the setting of the statue in tribute.

**5** At the Macartney Bridge turn left on to Baggot Street Lower, then right on Fitzwilliam Street Lower, and enter Merrion Square.

There are various plaques around the buildings of Merrion Square, including one for the poet W. B. Yeats, but the most prominent figure honoured here is Ireland's wittiest and most sparkling writer, Oscar Wilde (1854–1900). A rather louche-looking statue of the playwright and novelist lounges on a rock in the northwest corner of the gardens. Always a flamboyant figure, and a major presence in 19th-century literary circles, Wilde's plays such as *Lady Windermere's Fan* and his most popular work, *The Importance of Being Earnest*, are so slickly droll that it's often easy to overlook the fact that they deal with many social injustices of the day, notably women's rights. Famously tried and imprisoned for his homosexual affair with Lord Alfred Douglas ('Bosie'), Wilde's pitiful final days were spent alone and broke in Paris.

6 Leaving Merrion Square by the northwest corner, go down Clare Street and continue along Leinster Street South and Nassau Street, turning right at the top to the entrance gates of Trinity College on College Green.

Many literary alumni have entered the gates of Trinity College, including Bram Stoker and Oscar Wilde, and in the 1920s it was to be the temporary home of one of Ireland's great modernist playwrights, Samuel Beckett (1906–89), first as a student, then as a lecturer. Not the most accessible of writers, Beckett made his name in the 1950s with plays such as *Waiting for Godot* and *Endgame*.

7 With your back to the college gates, walk right up Westmoreland Street, over the river at O'Connell Bridge, and then right on to Eden Quay. Turn left on to Borough Street and then take the first right on to Abbey Street Lower.

Also known as the Irish National Theatre, the Abbey is something of a literary and theatrical institution in Dublin, and has been since the poet W. B. Yeats established it in 1904. Its opening coincided with the growing nationalist movement in Ireland as well as the Celtic Revival movement that saw a return to old folklore tales. As a result, many of its productions have been

## WHERE TO EAT

### ⦿ PLURABELLE BRASSERIE,
Earlsfort Terrace;
Tel: 676 5555.
Situated within The Conrad Hotel, the emphasis here is on good French-style brasserie dishes, served in elegant surroundings. €€€

### ⦿ TONER'S PUB,
139 Baggot Street Lower;
Tel: 676 3090.
One of Dublin's oldest pubs, dating from 1818, and the local of choice for poets W. B. Yeats and Patrick Kavanagh, there are few more atmospheric places to enjoy a pint of traditional Guinness. €

### ⦿ FLORIDITA,
Irish Life Mall, Abbey Street Lower;
Tel: 878 1032.
Everything is Cuban here – from music, to cigars, to food – and will have you tapping your toes as you sip on a mojito cocktail. €€

as much about Ireland and Irishness as they have been about theatre, premiering works such as Sean O'Casey's *Juno and the Paycock* in 1924 to Brian Friel's *Dancing at Lughnasa* in 1990. While it also stages international works as well as classics, the Abbey retains the same commitment to promoting Irish drama as it did in its earliest days.

**ABBEY THEATRE;**
www.abbeytheatre.ie

DOHENY & NESBITT'S PUB, BAGGOT STREET LOWER

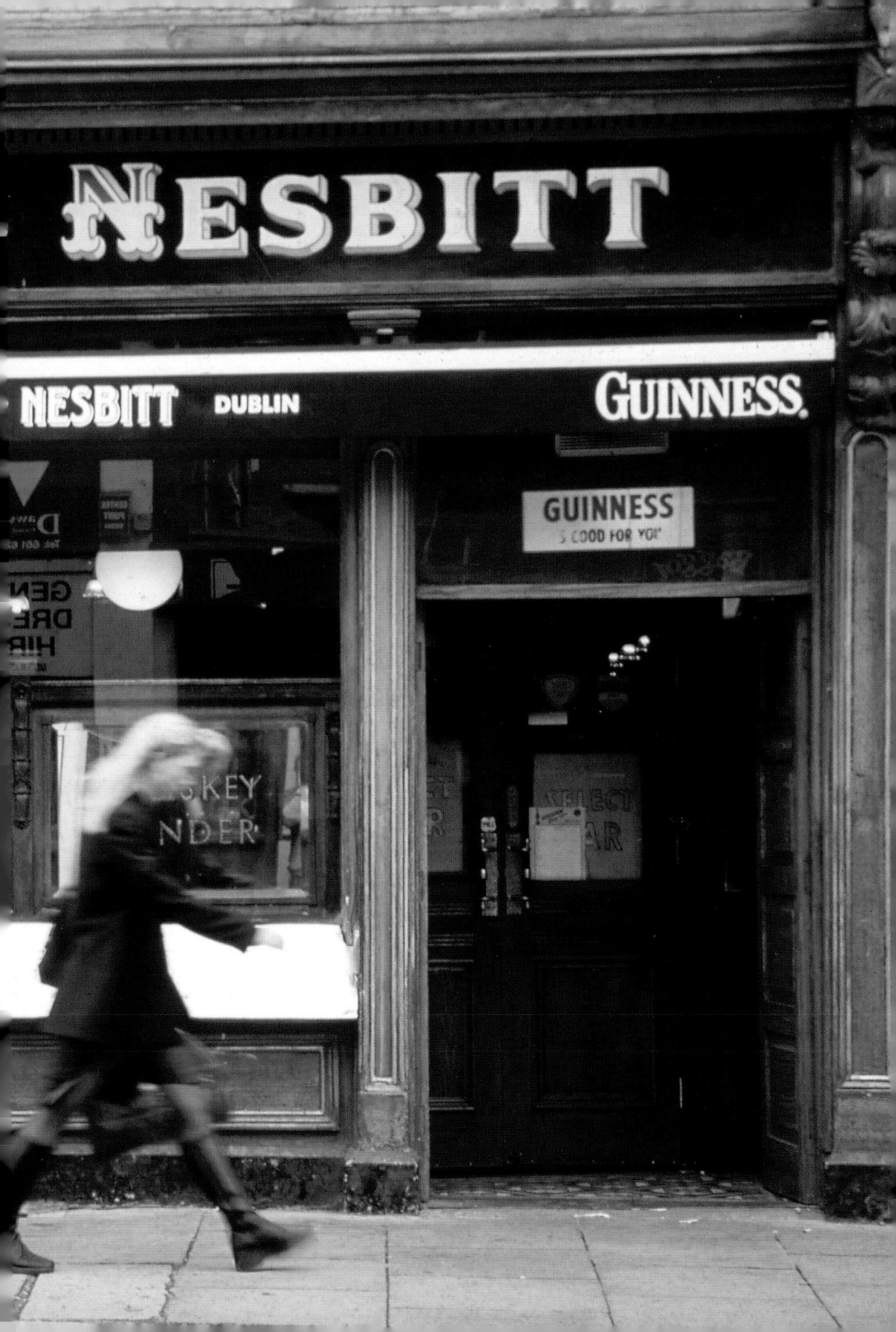
NESBITT
NESBITT DUBLIN
GUINNESS
GUINNESS

# A Pint of Plain is Your Only Man

**Dublin is a city full to the brim with legendary pubs, and almost all of them have a plethora of compelling stories to tell.**

Call it stout, porter or plain, or by its best-known brand name, Guinness – the thick black pint with the creamy head must be Dublin's best-known and best-loved export. But as any Dubliner will tell you, it's not the real thing unless it's brewed in Dublin from Liffey water. Accept no substitutes: as that master of the surreal, Flann O'Brien, also known as Myles na Gopaleen, put it in a memorable piece of doggerel, 'A pint of plain is your only man.' Except, of course, that even Dublin's most history-steeped pubs have moved with the times, and the drinks list is certain to offer New and Old World wines, imported beers and fancy cocktails as well as the time-honoured pint. How long you choose to spend on this exploration of Dublin's finest drinking places will obviously depend on how long you choose to spend in each pub, but it's probably inadvisable to attempt to down a pint at each step along the way.

Macartney Bridge carries Baggot Street across the Grand Canal. The name may conjure up visions of gondolas, but this rather depressing stretch of urban waterway is more commonly adorned with the rusting skeletons of shopping trolleys and stolen bicycles. Turn your back on it and walk up Baggot Street Lower to Doheny & Nesbitt at No. 5.

Doheny & Nesbitt looks as if it has been here forever, and the building it stands in is indeed more than 130 years old. The eponymous landlords hung up their sign here less than 50 years ago, but for at least half a century this has been the place where Ireland's politicians and spin-doctors come if they want to leak a story to a favoured journalist over a drink or two. Glass-panelled booths give patrons just the right amount of privacy for a privileged, off-the-record conversation. It is favoured by Dublin's legal eagles.

**2** Continue along Baggot Street Lower, lined with gracious townhouses (many of them with the bright-painted, brass-furnished doors that are emblematic of Georgian Dublin), and cross Lad Lane, Fitzwilliam Street Upper, Pembroke Street Lower and Ely Place, to Merrion Row and O'Donoghue's.

With its windows adorned with antique stout bottles, oil lanterns and other paraphernalia, O'Donoghue's resembles one of the franchised Irish pubs that have spread across the world like a creeping rash since the 1990s. But it has, in fact,

## WHERE TO EAT

**AYA,**
Clarendon Street;
Tel: 677 1544.
Try the sushi at this conveyor restaurant for a change from pub grub. Afternoon Happytime (Mon–Fri 2–7, Sat 3–7, Sun 1–7) is a bargain, with five sushi plates and one drink for €15. €

**THE PURTY KITCHEN,**
34/35 East Essex Street;
Tel: 677 0945.
The seafood chowder for which this restaurant is famous is a perfect energy-builder for walkers, but there are plenty more grill and seafood dishes on the menu. €€

**THE BRAZEN HEAD,**
20 Bridge Street;
Tel: 677 9549.
Good bar meals from 12.30 to 9, carvery lunches daily, à la carte menu every evening. €

been here for decades, and has a special place in the hearts of Irish folk music fans as the spot that gave folk pioneers The Dubliners their first regular gig, back in the 1950s. It still hosts informal folk sessions most evenings and weekends.

**3** Cross to the north side of Merrion Row, turn left on to St Stephen's Green North, then take the first right up Kildare Street with the National

93

**DISTANCE** 4 miles (7km)

**ALLOW** Half a day to all day, depending on how thirsty you are

**START** Macartney Bridge

**FINISH** South side of Father Mathew Bridge

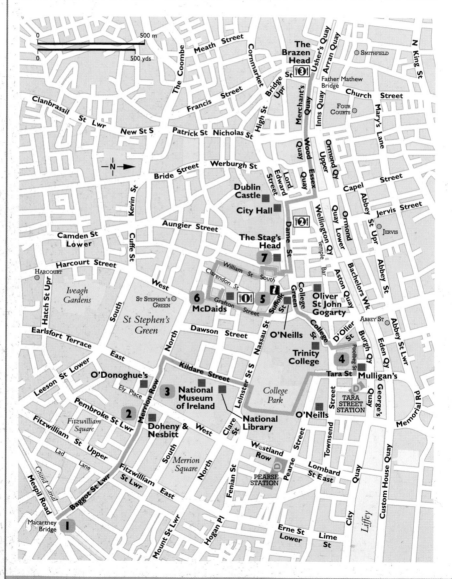

O'NEILL'S

M.J. O'NEILL

WINES   SPIRITS

Museum and National Library on your right, to Leinster Street. Cross the street to College Park, enter the park, and turn right to follow the footpath anticlockwise around the park to the north side. Turn left on Park Lane and follow it to its west end, where it runs right for a few paces to meet Pearse Street. Cross this main road and on the other side walk straight ahead up Tara Street, crossing Townsend Street, to the next corner. Turn left on Poolbeg Street and cross the street to the ochre-and-maroon frontage of Mulligan's, at No. 8.

John F. Kennedy is said to have enjoyed a pint here in honour of his Irish heritage when he visited Dublin in 1945. James Joyce was another visitor, and the pub gets more than one name-check in his work; he even named one of his characters in *Ulysses* after it. In Joyce's day, this was a proper Dublin working man's spit-and-sawdust pub, where a balanced diet was a drink in each hand and drinking was done standing up, to maximize the place's rascular density (defined as the number of rascals per square yard of floor space). It's a bit more civilized now – they even let women in – but it is still a classic example of a real Dublin boozer, with worn wood counter tops in abundance, and some say it has the best Guinness in the world.

**4** Leaving Mulligan's on your right, walk to the end of Poolbeg Street and go left on Hawkins Street. Walk down this very short street to Townsend Street, cross to the south side of College Street and turn left. With the west front of

Trinity College on your left, continue on the left side of College Green. This curves away from Trinity College. Turn left into Suffolk Street. O'Neill's is on the left, opposite the corner of Andrew Street and the tourist information office, at 121 Suffolk Street.

A triple-faced clock-cum-bar sign juts out from the first storey of this old red-brick pub, above a sturdy double-fronted window flanked by dark mahogany doors and dark-green woodwork picked out with white stucco embellishments. This pub has been known as O'Neill's since 1927, but it has been in existence for at least 300 years, and the site on which it stands has an even longer pedigree. Around 1,000 years ago it was the site of the Viking parliament called the Thing; in 1172, English King Henry II received the submission of many of the Irish chiefs on this same spot. And in the late 18th century, Arthur O'Connor published a newspaper from these premises in support of Wolfe Tone's United Irishmen and the failed rising of 1798.

**5** From O'Neills, cross Suffolk Street and turn left. At the next corner, turn right on to the west side of Grafton Street. Take the third turning on your right into Harry Street, a short, narrow street with McDaids at No. 3, across from the Westbury Hotel.

This is one of Dublin's great writers' pubs, with a grand Victorian front, all arches, stained glass and dark red paintwork, and a list of former clients that reads like a *Who's Who* of Irish literary reprobates of the 20th century, from Brendan Behan and Patrick Kavanagh to Flann O'Brien and J. P. Donleavy.

**6** Retrace your steps to the corner of Harry Street and Grafton Street and turn right. Take the next right down Chatham Street, cross the bottom of Clarendon Street on your right and then turn right up William Street South. Follow this street for two blocks to its north end and then turn left on Exchequer Street. Cross over to the north side, and take the next turning on your right into Dame Court.

The Stag's Head, at 1 Dame Court, is a grand example of Victorian pub design and a veritable drinker's palace, with its ceiling-high, gilt-trimmed mirrors on the walls, bull's-eye glass in the windows, and a massive marble bar top. James Joyce is said to have done some drinking here – but then every pub in Dublin seems to claim him as a former regular.

**7** Walk to the north end of Dame Court and the corner of Dame Lane. Turn left here, then almost immediately right to Dame Street. Cross the street, walk to the corner of Parliament Street (opposite City Hall) and turn right towards the river. When you reach the riverside, cross over, turn left and walk along first Essex Quay, then Wood Quay and finally Merchant's Quay. At the corner of Bridge Street, turn left to No. 20 and The Brazen Head.

The Brazen Head claims to be Dublin's oldest pub. The records show that there was a tavern here as early as 1198, but there have been a few changes over the last 800 years. There are traditional Irish music sessions every evening, so settle in for a well-earned pint or two at the end of this walk, or plan to get here on a Sunday for the regular afternoon session that kicks off around 12.30. Cross Father Mathew Bridge and turn right to follow the quays along the north bank of the Liffey and return to O'Connell Street.

# General Post Office to Glasnevin Cemetery

**Ireland is a country that produces more than its fair share of tragic history, but the events of 1916–1922 rank among the most unfortunate.**

By the first decade of the 20th century, the cause of Irish self-government had made great progress. In 1914 the British Parliament was on the verge of passing the Home Rule Bill, giving Ireland control over its own affairs. But with the outbreak of World War I, the government foolishly suspended this legislation. For some of the most radical and hot-headed campaigners of the Sinn Fein movement (the name means 'Ourselves Alone'), this was the last straw. They opted to take up arms in the hope that by attacking the British in Dublin they would trigger a spontaneous, nationwide uprising. The Easter Rising was, of course, a bloody failure. Up to its knees in the mud and blood of a war with Germany, Britain was in no mood to trifle with the amateur soldiers of the Irish Volunteers, and responded to the occupation of the General Post Office (where Padraig Pearse declared the Irish Republic), the Royal College of Surgeons and other key points with overwhelming force. The political and military struggle continued and turned into a short and fratricidal civil war that left long-lasting scars.

Start from the north side of St Stephen's Green and walk north up Dawson Street, keeping to the right-hand side, to a sturdy two-storey Georgian building about 150yards (135m) from the corner, on your right.

You could argue that this is where the modern Irish state was really born. Built in 1710, the Mansion House has been the residence of the Lord Mayor of Dublin since 1715, but on 21 January 1919 it was co-opted as the seat of the first Dáil Éireann (Irish Parliament), formed by the Sinn Fein MPs who won a landslide victory in the elections of 1918 but refused to take their seats in the British Parliament at Westminster. From here, Michael Collins (1890–1922), the former post office worker who became the Dáil's Éireann's Minister of Finance, also directed the Irish Volunteers in an urban guerrilla campaign against the British. When the British brought in a crack team of undercover Special Branch officers, Collins traced them and had 14 of them assassinated. British reprisals only hardened support for Sinn Fein, but in 1921 a ceasefire was called and the Anglo-Irish Treaty created the Irish Free State. But the treaty did not go far enough for radical Republicans; within a year, they and the new Free State government were embroiled in civil war. Mansion House is not open to the public.

2 Continue for three blocks to the north end of Dawson Street. Cross Nassau Street and turn right. Go along Nassau Street with College Park on

## WHERE TO EAT

### 🍴 FIRE,
Mansion House, Dawson Street; Tel: 676 7200.
Glamorous restaurant next to the Mansion House, with indoor and outdoor dining, modern American and European menu, glitzy interior and Ireland's first wood-burning pizza oven. €€€

### 🍴 PORTERHOUSE NORTH,
North Cross Guns Bridge; Tel: 830 9922.
This big, trendy art deco style pub spreads over four floors, with outside seating out back and in front. Tasty pizzas and a good choice of beers. €

### 🍴 IL CORVO,
98–100 Drumcondra Street Upper; Tel: 837 5727.
Solid, slightly old-fashioned trattoria serving good solid traditional Italian cooking. Bring a hearty appetite, as portions are generous. €€

your left, continue along Leinster Street South and turn left into Lincoln Place. At the end of Lincoln Place turn left on to Westland Row. Follow this to its north end (with Pearse Station on the corner). Cross Pearse Street and turn left. Take the second on your right, Shaw Street, and walk north for one block to Townsend Street. Cross, and continue north on Moss Street to the riverside. Cross the Liffey to the north bank.

99

DISTANCE **3 miles (4.8km)**

ALLOW **2 hours**

START **Corner of St Stephen's Green North and St Stephen's Green West**

FINISH **Glasnevin Cemetery South Gate**

While walking across the bridge, admire the grand front of the Custom House beneath its green copper dome. Walk left along to Eden Quay, turn right into O'Connell Street.

James Gandon, who designed the Custom House as well as many other Dublin landmarks, would be pleased to see his building looking so spruce more than 200 years after it was completed, in 1791. It has always been underused, and in 1921, with Sinn Fein fighters and British troops skirmishing in Dublin's streets and a self-declared Sinn Fein government sitting in the Mansion House, Sinn Fein sympathizers torched this little-loved symbol of British rule. It burned for five days, and it wasn't completely restored until 1991.

**3** From Eden Quay, cross to the left-hand side of O'Connell Street for one short block to the bullet-scarred façade of the General Post Office. Turn left into the main hall of the building.

The statue that dominates the main hall is the heroic warrior of Celtic myth, Cúchulainn, who was said to be so agile that he could turn around inside his own skin. Cúchulainn was the right-hand man of the legendary king Finn MacCool. The statue symbolizes the contingent of Republican volunteers who held out for six days here, led by James Connolly and Padraig Pearse, while being shelled by British artillery and gunboats. 'A terrible beauty is born', wrote W. B. Yeats of the Easter Rising. But then, he wasn't there getting shot at. At least the 64 freedom

ABOVE: THE CUSTOM HOUSE, A LANDMARK BUILDING BY JAMES GANDON

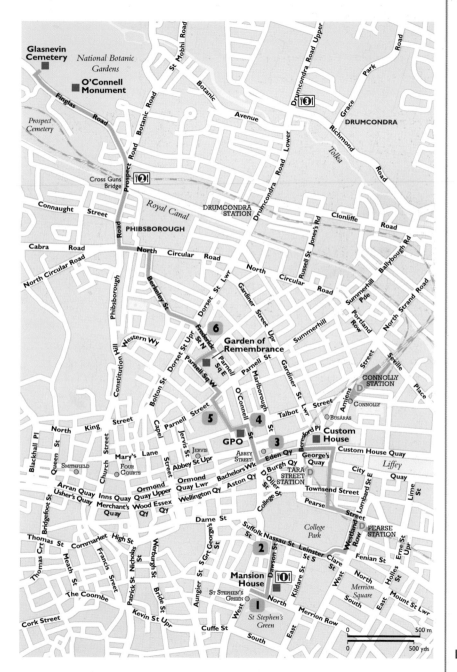

Glasnevin
Cemetery

National Botanic
Gardens

O'Connell
Monument

Prospect
Cemetery

Finglas        Road

St Mobhi Road

Botanic        Road

Botanic

Avenue

DRUMCONDRA

Grace        Park        Road

Drumcondra Road Upper

Richmond        Road

Tolka

Cross Guns
Bridge

Prospect Road

Royal Canal

DRUMCONDRA
STATION

Drumcondra Road Lower

Clonliffe        Road

Connaught        Street

PHIBSBOROUGH

North        Circular        Road

North        Circular        Road

Ballybough Rd

Cabra        Road

North Circular Road

Phibsborough        Road

Phibsborough

Berkeley St

Dorset St Upr

Frederick St N

Dorset St Upr

Western Wy

Parnell Sq W

6

Garden of
Remembrance

Parnell
Sq E

Parnell        Sq N

Marlborough        Street

Gardiner        Street        Upr

Summerhill

Summerhill        Pde

Portland        Row

North        Strand        Road

Russell St        Jones's Rd

Seville        Place

CONNOLLY
STATION

Amiens        Street

Constitution Hill

Bolton St

Parnell        Street

Capel        Street

O'Connell        Street

Talbot        Street        Lwr

CONNOLLY

BUSÁRAS

Seville

North        King        Street

Jervis St

JERVIS

5

Parnell        Street

GPO

4

3

Beresford Pl

Custom
House

Custom House Quay

Blackhall Pl

Queen        St

SMITHFIELD

Church        Street

Mary's        Lane

FOUR
COURTS

Abbey St Upr

ABBEY
STREET

Eden Qy

Burgh Qy

George's
Quay

City        Quay

Liffey

Arran Quay

Inns Quay

Ormond
Quay Upper

Ormond
Quay Lwr

Bachelors Wk

Aston Qy

Oliver

TARA
STREET
STATION

Townsend        Street

Lombard St E

Lime        St

Usher's Quay

Merchant's
Quay

Wood Essex
Qy

Qy

Wellington Qy

College St

Pearse

Bridgefoot St

Thomas        Crt

Cornmarket

High St

Dame        St

Francis        Street

Gt George's St

Suffolk
St

Nassau St

College
Park

Leinster
St S

Pearse        Street

Westland        Row

PEARSE
STATION

Erne St        Upr

Thomas        St

Meath        St

Patrick St

Nichols        St

Werburgh St

Bride St

Aungier        St

ST STEPHEN'S
GREEN

2

Dawson        St

Clare
St S

Fenian St

North

Merrion
Square

South

Holles        St

Mount St Lwr

The        Coombe

Kevin St Upr

Mansion
House

1

St Stephen's
Green

North

Merrion Row

West

Kildare        St

East

Cork        Street

Cuffe        St

South

East

0        500 m

0        500 yds

**14**

fighters who died in the six days of fighting were volunteers, while most of the 130 British soldiers who were killed were regular army professionals. The 300 or more civilian casualties had less say in the matter, and the instigators of the rising were popularly reviled for causing their deaths. But the execution of Connolly, Pearse and other ringleaders turned them into martyrs.

**4** Walk past the General Post Office on your left, and turn left into Henry Street. Pass Henry Place, almost immediately on your right from the corner, and take the next right on to Moore Street. Weekdays, this is a busy and colourful flower, fruit and vegetable market. No. 16 Moore Street is on the right-hand side, just north of the corner.

A grey plaque on the wall of this unassuming brick building records (in Irish) that this was where the flame of the Easter Rising finally guttered out. On 28 April 1916, with the GPO in ruins, the members of the self-declared Provisional Government withdrew to Moore Street. The following day, Pearse sent a young nurse, Elizabeth O'Farrell, to the British commander, General Lowe, with his surrender. Plans to demolish the building raised protest: No. 16 is now to be listed as a national monument, with plans to turn it into an interpretation centre telling the story of the rising.

**5** Walk up Moore Street to Parnell Street, cross to the north side, walk down Parnell Square West and turn right to enter the Garden of Remembrance at the north end of Parnell Square.

This poignant little park is laden with memories of Irish freedom fighters. After the surrender of the Provisional

ABOVE: GARDEN OF REMEMBRANCE; OPPOSITE: A CELTIC CROSS, GLASNEVIN CEMETERY

Government, its leaders were held overnight here before being taken to Kilmainham Gaol, where Pearse, Connolly and five other signatories of the declaration of the Republic were tried for treason by a kangaroo court, convicted, and shot. In all, more than 90 people were sentenced to death by British courts in the aftermath of the rising and more than a thousand were jailed as sympathizers with the rebels. The garden was dedicated as a memorial in 1966, on the 50th anniversary of the Easter Rising. The pool in the centre of the garden is decorated with a mosaic of broken weapons, symbolizing an end to war.

**6** Go to the northeast corner of Parnell Square, turn left, and walk along Frederick Street North to Dorset Street. Cross, and walk up Blessington Street, immediately opposite Frederick Street North. After one block, turn right on Berkeley Street, which curves north to the North Circular Road. Cross this busy main road and walk west along it until you turn right on Phibsborough Road. Walk north for three short blocks to the Cross Guns Bridge, and cross the Royal Canal and the railway line running parallel to it. After one block of Prospect Road, at a Y-junction fork left on Finglas Road. Ahead to your right is Glasnevin Cemetery. Enter by the southeast gate.

This is the last resting place of a veritable roll-call of freedom fighters – including Daniel O'Connell – but it's less gloomy than it sounds, as much of its 47 acres (19ha) is taken up by rose beds, glasshouses and botanic gardens. Opened in 1832, the cemetery has four grand Victorian gateways and a vast array of equally grand tombstones and monuments. The last hero of the war of independence to be buried here was Kevin Barry (1902–20), whose body was disinterred from nearby Mountjoy Prison in October 2001. Barry was hanged in Mountjoy for murder after being captured when his guerrilla squad ambushed a British army lorry in 1920. Three British soldiers died. Barry was taken prisoner after his pistol jammed. He was offered a reprieve in return for the names of his comrades, but refused, and was executed on 1 November 1920, aged 18.
**GLASNEVIN CEMETERY;**
www.glasnevin-cemetery.ie

GREAT PALM HOUSE, NATIONAL BOTANIC GARDENS, GLASNEVIN

# The Fury of the Norsemen

**The River Liffey drew Norse and Danish raiders and settlers to this part of the world, and the heart of Viking Dublin lies beneath Wood Quay.**

The first Vikings blew in around AD841, and they came to stay, intermarrying with the ruling families of Celtic Ireland and eventually even accepting Christianity. The Irish called them the *Gall* – 'the fair-haired foreigners' – and you can still see their genetic legacy in Dublin. The Vikings have had a bad press for more than 1,000 years: Irish, Scottish and English monks used to pray to the Lord to be spared from 'the fury of the Norsemen'. The Vikings found the treasures of the defenceless island monasteries of Ireland, Scotland and England impossible to resist and pillaged them frequently from the 8th century onwards. The Christian church had a virtual monopoly on the flow of information and the written word in medieval Europe, and could hardly be expected to give the raiders anything but an evil reputation. But Dublin owes its foundation and many of its treasures to them. Archaeologists managed to glean a treasure-trove of artefacts and information from the Wood Quay site on the South Bank before Dublin Corporation built its offices over the ancient Viking foundations.

1 Your landmark at the beginning of this walk is Christ Church Cathedral, which stands on the north side of Christ Church Place. From here, cross to the north side of the High Street and take the second right (after Winetavern Street) into St Michael's Hill, then turn right to enter Dublinia and The Viking World.

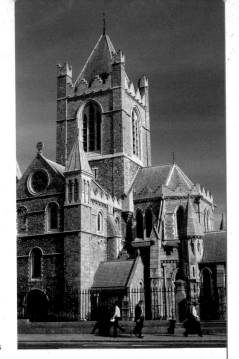

Based on archaeological excavations along the Liffey at Wood Quay, this exhibition uses audiovisual displays, multimedia presentations, reconstructions and artefacts from the site to bring Viking Dublin to life, making it clear that the Vikings were much more than just bloodthirsty pirates. A street of houses as they would have looked in Viking times is one of the highlights, along with displays of weapons, coins, jewellery, tools, textiles and household goods found at the Wood Quay site. More Viking relics are on show at the National Museum, which we'll visit later on this walk.

**DUBLINIA AND THE VIKING WORLD;**

www.dublinia.ie

2 Retrace your steps to the north side of Christ Church Place and the entrance to the cathedral.

Dublin's oldest building, with its blend of Romanesque and Gothic architecture, stands on the site of a wooden cathedral erected by Sidric, the Viking ruler of Dublin, in 1038. Also called Sigtrygg or Sedriug, and nicknamed 'Silkbeard', Sidric married the daughter of the Irish King Brian Boru, who in the early years of the second millennium had almost succeeded in uniting Ireland under his sway. Brian, in turn, married Sidric's widowed mother, making him Sidric's stepfather as well as his father-in-law. This didn't stop Sidric allying with Mael Morda, King of Leinster, against Brian in 1014. Sidric, Mael Morda and their allies met Brian's army at Clontarf, just north of Dublin. In the confused battle that followed, almost all the leaders were killed, including Brian, but Sidric watched from a distance and survived. Clontarf has gone down in history as a great Irish victory over the Vikings, but in fact Vikings fought on both sides, and canny Sidric lived on to rule Dublin until his death 28 years later.

**CHRIST CHURCH CATHEDRAL;**

www.cccdub.ie

**DISTANCE** 1.6 miles (2.5km)

**ALLOW** 3 hours

**START** Christ Church Cathedral, Christ Church Place

**FINISH** National Museum of Ireland, Kildare Street

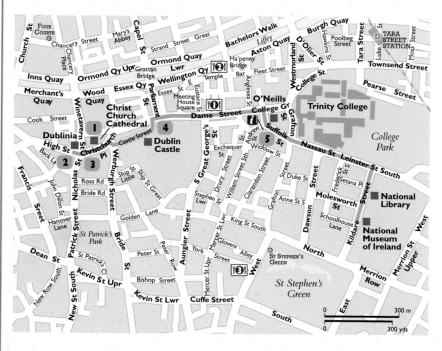

**3** Cross to the south side of Christ Church Place, and where it joins Werburgh Street and Castle Street walk straight ahead on Castle Street. At the end of this street, where it meets Cork Hill, turn right to enter Dublin Castle.

Located where a smaller river, the Poddle, flowed into the Liffey to form a handy anchorage, this was a natural place for the Vikings to build a stronghold. Remnants of this early Viking fortress can be seen in the Undercroft, below the much more

substantial castle begun in 1205 and added to over centuries of English rule. Ironically, Strongbow's Anglo-Normans, whose arrival on the scene spelt the end of Viking Ireland, were themselves the descendants of Danish Vikings who had sailed south to settle in Normandy. It is still not certain what triggered the sudden eruption of Scandinavian seafarers from the fjords of Denmark and Norway around the 8th century AD. Population pressure and climate change are possible factors. What is certain is that

the Viking presence plugged Ireland into a wide-ranging Norse-Celtic culture that ultimately stretched all the way to the Scottish Hebrides, Orkney, Shetland, and Iceland as well as Scandinavia. Some Vikings even got as far as Constantinople to serve in the Varangir Guard as bodyguards of the Byzantine Emperor.
**DUBLIN CASTLE;**

www.dublincastle.ie

**4** Leaving the castle on Cork Hill, turn right on to the south side of Dame Street, cross over Great George's Street and Trinity Street, and just after Dame Street merges into College Green, turn right into Suffolk Street, where a

conspicuous pub, O'Neill's, is on the left at No. 121, opposite the tourist information office.

There is at least some evidence that in Dublin's Viking heyday, this was the site of the Thingmount, where the Viking Parliament, or Thing, came together to elect rulers, try criminals, decide titles to land or resolve a blood feud. Some decisions were put to a mass vote (women and slaves, or *thralls*, didn't get a voice), others were decided by a panel of respected judges. The Vikings are often portrayed as barbarians, but they had a high respect for their own version of law, justice and democracy. The Thingmount

was an artificial earthen mound 40ft (12m) high and 240ft (73m) round. Sadly, it was levelled in 1681, when its earth and stones were used to raise the level of flood-prone Nassau Street nearby. A handful of weapons and other finds discovered are in the National Museum, but much more must have been lost.

5 With the pub on your left, go to the end of Suffolk Street, continue along Nassau Street, passing Dawson Street, Fredrick Street and Nassau Place on your right, and turn right into Kildare Street. Take the left-hand side, past the National Library, and enter the wrought-iron gates of the National Museum of Ireland – Archaeology and History.

The National Museum's archaeology collection contains a treasury of Viking and Norse-Irish art, and if further proof were to be needed of the civilizing mission of the Vikings in Ireland, here it is. Not only Dublin, but virtually every Irish seaport city has Viking roots (the ancient Irish were neither great town-builders nor keen seafarers). The museum's Viking Ireland collection spans the period from the earliest Viking contacts with the Irish, beginning around AD800, up to the coming of the Anglo-Normans in the mid-12th century. There are grave goods from Viking funerary sites, for, happily for present-day archaeologists, the Vikings hoped to take wealth and weapons with them into the afterlife. Discoveries from settlements all over Ireland show a gentler side of their life as farmers and homesteaders, and the

## WHERE TO EAT

🍽 OLIVER GOLDSMITH'S BAR,
Trinity Arch Hotel,
46–49 Dame Street;
Tel: 679 4455.
Rambling pub roughly midway between Dublin Castle and Trinity College; a good place for basic pub grub and a drink. €

🍽 QUAYS BAR,
11 Temple Bar;
Tel: 679 3922.
Small, friendly pub in the heart of Temple Bar with a cosy restaurant upstairs. €

🍽 SHANAHAN'S ON THE GREEN,
119 St Stephen's Green;
Tel: 407 0939.
This recent addition to the Dublin dining scene serves an American-style surf-and-turf menu in immaculate Georgian surroundings. €€€

magnificently ornate silver ornaments show a culture with a sophisticated sense of style and great metalworking skill. The finds from the Dublin digs carried out between 1962 and 1981 comprise Europe's finest collection of discoveries from an early medieval town, and the final section, with its outstanding church silver from the 11th and 12th centuries, shows the last flowering of the unique Celtic-Scandinavian culture.

**NATIONAL MUSEUM OF IRELAND;**
www.museum.ie

# Dublin's City Centre Music Venues

**As it does in so many ways, Dublin punches well above its weight when it comes to music, and its musical legends leave a trail worth following.**

This walk takes you round some iconic spots associated with the rock, pop and folk artists who began their careers here. From the inventive, jazzy, hard-rocking Thin Lizzy and the edgy, punk-influenced sarcasm of the Boom Town Rats in the 1970s, to the soppy soft rock of Chris de Burgh, the self-lacerating oeuvre of Sinéad O'Connor and the outright kitsch of Riverdance, Ireland's capital has contributed stellar talent to every strand of popular music for more than four decades. Some of them – like rock legend U2 – have gone global while keeping their Dublin roots (and indeed expanding them by using their rock dollars to buy up prime city properties). Others, like old-school folkies The Dubliners, never really left (except to go on tour). Dublin has, of course, been a foot-tapping city of music from its earliest beginnings, and there are plenty of pubs that host an impromptu acoustic jam session most nights of the week.

From the south side of Wellington Quay, opposite Grattan Bridge, walk eastward to the Clarence Hotel, which faces the Liffey, at 6–8 Wellington Quay.

Built in 1852, the Clarence was given a facelift in the 1930s but grew shabbier over the next four decades. By the 1970s it was looking decidedly down at heel, but its bar had become popular with the young guns of the nascent bohemian Temple Bar scene – among them a group of musicians who would go on to mega-star status. They were Bono and The Edge, and U2, the band that they formed with Adam Clayton and Larry Mullen, became the biggest musical phenomenon ever to come out of Dublin. By 1992, with a portfolio of hugely successful hits, Bono and The Edge were wealthy enough to buy their old haunt and convert it into a glamorous boutique hotel that has become the favoured Dublin address for visiting celebs. The band recorded *Beautiful Day* here for the BBC's *Top of the Pops* in September 2000.
**CLARENCE HOTEL;**
www.theclarence.ie

2 Continue along Wellington Quay to No. 42, on your right next to Ha'penny Bridge.

The Ha'penny Bridge Inn, at 42 Wellington Quay, was a favourite watering-hole for the members of Thin Lizzy in the early years of their career, and an original photo of Phil Lynott still has a place of honour on its crowded walls. Thin Lizzy exploded onto the world stage in 1973 with a sound totally unlike anything that had ever come out of Ireland – a country that until then had been pretty much associated with the old-style folk music and 'rebel songs' of bands like The Dubliners or The Clancy Brothers. With his afro hair and tight black leathers, Lynott was Ireland's first classic rock cowboy. His mixed ancestry – his African-Brazilian father left his Irish mother soon after Phil was born in 1949 – gave him an even greater exotic appeal. Thin Lizzy's first big hit, *Whiskey in the Jar* (1973) took an old Irish folk ballad and turned it into a rock anthem, while the swaggering lyrics of *The Boys are Back in Town* became their greatest hit. Sadly, Phil Lynott did not handle success well. Drug and alcohol abuse ruined his health and destroyed his creative abilities, and he died young, in 1986. For a generation of fans, though, Thin Lizzy's music lives on.

OPPOSITE: A JAM SESSION AT THE OLIVER ST JOHN GOGARTY; ABOVE: THE CLARENCE HOTEL

DISTANCE **2 miles (3.5km)**

ALLOW **2 hours**

START **Grattan Bridge (Wellington Quay)**

FINISH **O'Donoghues, Merrion Row**

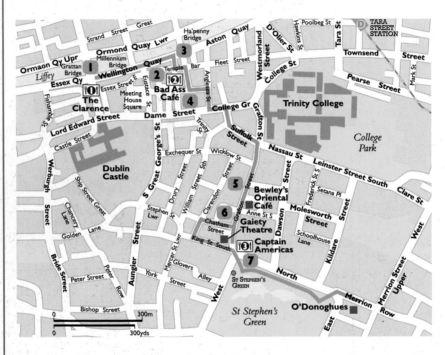

**3** Turn right down Fownes Street Lower, then left on to Temple Bar. Take the next right into Crown Alley.

The Bad Ass Café, at 9–11 Crown Alley, opened in 1983 and quickly became one of the hubs of the Temple Bar scene. Among the service staff was a young woman named Sinéad O'Connor, then working her way through college at Dublin's School of Music while song writing and performing with a new Dublin band, Ton Ton Macoute. Born

in 1966, the shaven-headed warbler was destined to become a world star, gaining a reputation as an outspoken critic of targets ranging from Pope John Paul II to American foreign policy, and even fellow Dublin musicians U2 – whose music she denounced as 'bombastic' – while defending the aims of the Irish Republican Army. In 2003 she retired from the music business and was ordained into the Tridentine Church, a small religious movement, taking the name Bernadette to signal a change of

direction in her life. She's not the Bad Ass's only rock connection – U2 and Bruce Springsteen have also dropped in to sample one of the legendary burgers.

**4** Continue up Crown Alley, turn left on to Cope Street and then right on to Anglesea Street. Continue to the junction of Dame Street and College Green. Cross Dame Street, walk past Trinity Lane, turn right into Suffolk Street, then at the corner of Suffolk Street and Grafton Street turn right down Grafton Street to No. 78–79, Bewley's Oriental Café.

It's a little difficult to picture Dublin's punk legends sitting over a cup of tea in these genteel, old-fashioned surroundings. Bewley's has been at this address since the mid-19th century, supplying self-service tea, coffee, scones and sandwiches. But Bewley's is where Bob Geldof penned *Rat Trap* for the Boom Town Rats – the first ever single from an Irish rock band to go to number one in the British charts. The Rats disbanded in 1986 after a massive 10-year career, and Geldof is now better known as a campaigner.

**5** Back out on Grafton Street, turn left and continue down the street to Captain Americas, at No. 44.

Soft-rock star Chris de Burgh, best known for his hit single *Lady in Red*, began his singing career at Captain Americas while studying at nearby Trinity College in the early 1970s. Captain Americas first opened in 1971, and has hardly changed since then. Born in Argentina, Chris de Burgh is apparently

very popular there – perhaps even more so than in Dublin.

6 Backtrack up Grafton Street and go left into Chatham Street. At the end of this street, turn left on Clarendon Street, then left again to the Gaiety Theatre, on the left midway along King Street South, a very grand building with a decorative, Venetian-style brick façade.

Known as the 'Grand Old Lady of South King Street', the Gaiety was built by two enterprising brothers, John and Michael Gunn, who commissioned C. J. Phipps to design a theatre in the style of a grand European opera house. It was erected in record time – just over six months from start to finish – and opened on 27 November 1871 with a performance of Oliver Goldsmith's *She Stoops to Conquer*. The Gaiety has been a venue for some of the greatest stars of opera, ballet and theatre – Anna Pavlova, Joan Sutherland and Peter O'Toole among them – as well as singers such as Sinéad O'Connor and Dublin's best-known outspoken radical singer-songwriter, Christy Moore.

**GAIETY THEATRE;**
www.gaietytheatre.ie

7 Follow King Street to the northwest corner of St Stephen's Green and stroll through the park to the Merrion Square gateway. Cross St Stephen's Green East to Merrion Row, then walk on to O'Donoghues at 15 Merrion Row.

This folksy pub, with folk-music sessions every night, is a place of pilgrimage for

## WHERE TO EAT

**⌷◉⌷ THE TEAROOM AT THE CLARENCE,**
Clarence Hotel, 6–8 Wellington Quay;
Tel: 407 0813.
www.theclarence.ie
The two-course market menu emphasizes fresh, seasonal Irish-sourced produce and is excellent value for money. €€/€€€

**⌷❷⌷ BAD ASS CAFÉ,**
9–11 Crown Alley;
Tel: 671 2596.
The best burgers in Dublin, plus pasta, steak, pizzas and great chilli, fajitas and other Mexican classics. €€

**⌷❸⌷ CAPTAIN AMERICAS,**
44 Grafton Street;
Tel: 671 5266.
The restaurant that brought real American burgers to Dublin also serves excellent steaks, salads, Cajun chicken and a choice of vegetarian dishes. €€

Irish traditional music fans. This was where the legendary folk band The Dubliners was formed in 1962. They went on to become pioneers of the Irish traditional music revival that eventually spread far beyond Dublin. To return to the city centre walk back to St Stephen's Green North, cross over and walk north up Kildare Street from where you can catch buses 7 or 7A to Burgh Quay or 10, 11, 13 to O'Connell Street.

117

STAINED-GLASS WINDOWS ARE A FEATURE AT BEWLEY'S ORIENTAL CAFÉ

# Multi-ethnic Dublin

**A generation ago, Dublin was an overwhelmingly white, Irish and Catholic city, but it has now become a much more cosmopolitan place.**

Phil Lynott, front man of Ireland's rock band Thin Lizzy (see Walk 16), claimed to be the first-ever black Dubliner. Today there are Dubliners with roots in Thailand, China, Pakistan, Nigeria, Somalia, Ethiopia, South Africa, the Middle East, Greece, Turkey, and the 'new EU' nations of central and Eastern Europe, to name just a few. In an older sense, of course, Dublin has always been a multi-ethnic city. Founded by Scandinavians, settled by Anglo-Normans and their French followers, the city's later immigrants included, in the 17th century, French Huguenots fleeing persecution in Catholic France and substantial numbers of Jewish people from mainland Europe. Ireland's own Travellers, with a lifestyle similar to the European Roma folk and speaking a distinctive, archaic dialect of Gaelic, are also a presence. In recent decades Ireland has also accepted significant numbers of asylum seekers from war-torn regions such as the Balkans. This walk explores some of the landmarks of Dublin's multicultural history.

1 At the north end of O'Connell Street, on the left-hand side as you face north to Parnell Square, turn left onto Parnell Street, pausing to salute 'the uncrowned King of Ireland', whose memorial stands here.

The Parnell Monument, commemorating Charles Stuart Parnell, presides over the crossroads of O'Connell Street and Parnell Street. Although he was the greatest campaigner for Home Rule of the second half of the 19th century, Parnell, like a number of other prominent Home Rule leaders then and later, was a Protestant; the cause of Irish independence was not a sectarian struggle. It attracted a cosmopolitan following, with Scottish and Welsh guiding lights as well as native Irish leaders and Anglo-Irishmen like Sir Roger Casement (hanged for his part in the Easter Rising) and Erskine Childers, while the Sinn Fein leader Eamon de Valera was, as his name suggests, of Spanish descent.

2 Continue along Parnell Street and, with the Rotunda Hospital on your right on the opposite side of the street, pass Moore Lane on your left, and turn left into Moore Street.

Packed with fruit and vegetable stalls and flower sellers all day except Sunday, and lined with small greengrocers' shops and delicatessens, Moore Street Market vividly reflects the tastes of an increasingly cosmopolitan population. Next to stalls piled with potatoes, carrots, onions and other homily there are

heaps more exotic offerings from the Mediterranean, Asia and even Africa: kiwi fruit, aubergines, sweet potatoes, pak choi, mangoes and more.

3 At the foot of Moore Street, turn right on to Henry Street. After one block, take the first left on to Upper Liffey Street. After one block, cross Abbey Street Upper to Liffey Street Lower and walk down to Ormond Quay Lower and the riverside, where the Ha'penny Bridge crosses the river. Turn right, staying on the north side of the street with the river on the opposite side, and walk towards Jervis Street.

The north side of Ormond Street Lower is now occupied by Dublin's 'Italian Quarter', a newly built eating and shopping district also known as 'Quartier Bloom'. Designed by Mick Wallace, it's

OPPOSITE: MOORE STREET MARKET; ABOVE: PARNELL MONUMENT

DISTANCE  **3 miles (4.8km)**

ALLOW  **2–3 hours**

START  **Corner of Parnell Street (south side) and O'Connell Street**

FINISH  **South Circular Road opposite Victoria Street**

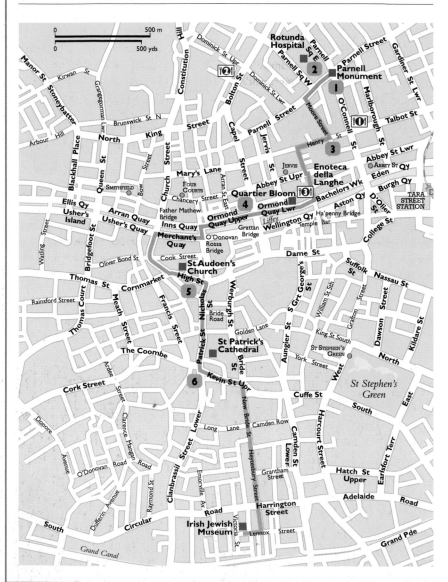

OPPOSITE: ST AUDOEN'S CHURCH

perhaps not as authentically Italian as it claims to be, but it does have several outstanding Italian restaurants and food shops, including Bar Italia, run by Dublin-Italian restaurateurs Izzo and Crescenzi.

**4** Continue along Ormond Quay with the river on your left, past Grattan Bridge. At O'Donovan Rossa Bridge, next left, cross the Liffey to Merchant's Quay and turn right. At Father Mathew Bridge, turn left on to Bridge Street Lower and walk to Bridge Street Upper and then to the corner of Cornmarket. Turn left to enter the pretty churchyard of St Audoen's Church, at the corner of Cornmarket and High Street.

Recently restored, St Audoen's is virtually two churches in one. The earlier church, closest to the corner, is the oldest surviving church in the city, with a 12th-century tower that is claimed to be Ireland's oldest, though its bells and nave date from the 15th century. Behind the church is St Audoen's Arch, the only surviving gateway of several that formed part of the old city walls. The church is named after St Ouen, patron saint of Normandy and 7th-century bishop of Rouen, indicating its Anglo-Norman antecedents. Next to the medieval church is a much newer addition, St Audoen's Catholic Church, completed in 1848. Its great bell, nicknamed 'The Liberator' after Daniel O'Connell, tolled to celebrate his release from jail in 1843, and seven years later to mourn his death.

**ST AUDOEN'S CHURCH;**
www.sacred-destinations.com/ireland/dublin-st-audoen-church.htm

**5** Continue along High Street with the twin churches behind you on your left. At the end of High Street, turn right on to Nicholas Street. At the end of Nicholas Street, continue straight on down Patrick Street, with St Patrick's Cathedral on your left.

St Patrick is another multi-ethnic Irishman; according to legend, he was

born in Christian Wales, was captured by Viking slave-traders and sold in Ireland, bringing his faith with him. His charisma brought him converts, and he started baptizing them here around AD450.

**ST PATRICK'S CATHEDRAL;**

www.stpatrickscathedral.ie

**6** At the south end of Patrick Street, turn left on to Kevin Street Upper, walk to the end and turn right on New Bride Street. Follow this to its south end, where it becomes Heytesbury Street. Continue to the South Circular Road. Cross this busy main road and walk on down to Stamer Street. After one block, at Lennox Street, turn right, cross small Kingsland Park Avenue on to Walworth Road and almost immediately turn right, to the Irish Jewish Museum at No. 3.

This former synagogue was reborn as a museum dedicated to the history of Irish Jewry in 1985, and was officially opened by the then President of Israel, the Irish-born Chaim Herzog. The museum traces the Herzog family tree, and includes a plethora of pictures, photos, books and documents from the Jewish community, from its heyday in the mid-19th century to the present day. Ireland's Jewish community has dwindled, mainly due to emigration since the founding of the state of Israel in 1948, but Jewish professionals, writers and educators played a significant role in Irish culture and history both before and after independence. Dublin also provided a refuge from the Nazis for Ernst Schrödinger, the German-Jewish pioneer of quantum mechanics, whose

## WHERE TO EAT

**|O| BESHOFF,**
5–6 O'Connell Street;
Tel: 872 4400.
Dublin's top fish and chip restaurant with superbly fresh fish, crispy, chunky chips and a choice of condiments and sauces from salt and vinegar to garlic and curry. €

**|O| TRANSYLVANIA ROMANIAN TAVERN,**
Henrietta Street;
Tel: 874 0407.
This is a home from home for Dublin's Romanian expatriates, with a menu that is heavy on hearty, meaty stews and grills, and entertainment from a resident Romanian band. €

**|O| ENOTECA DELLA LANGHE,**
Bloom's Lane;
Tel: 888 0834.
Bright new wine shop and wine bar with 150 different wines from northern Italy in its cellars, 15 different wines by the glass each week, and bruschetta, cold cuts and cheese to sample. €€

'cat in the box' thought-experiment to illustrate one of his more arcane hypotheses is a triumph of scientific surrealism. Walk to the corner of Victoria Street and the South Circular Road to catch a bus back to the centre.

**IRISH JEWISH MUSEUM;**

www.jewishireland.org

# Shopping: Smithfield to the South Side

**Ireland's booming 'Celtic tiger' economy of the 1990s turned Dublin into a top shopping city, with world-class designer outlets and art galleries.**

As well as the modern malls and shopping centres that have made their appearance north and south of the river, there are older shops where you can browse for Victorian and Georgian antiques, vintage clothing and accessories, Irish gold, silver and enamelwork inspired by ancient Celtic designs, linen and crystal glassware, bone china, tweeds and knitwear. Dublin's traditional outdoor markets are also still thriving. Some of them, such as Smithfield, have been doing business on the same spot for centuries. Others, such as Moore Street, have moved with the times and expanded their range of produce to include a plethora of exotic goods that reflects the changing tastes of Dubliners.

From the corner of Arran Quay and Church Street (opposite the north end of Father Mathew Bridge and next to the Four Courts) on the north bank of the Liffey, walk west along the north side of Arran Quay. Turn right on to Arran Street and walk up this short, small street onto the wide, cobbled rectangle of Smithfield.

The best time to visit this market square is on the first Sunday of each month, when it is the venue for the horse and pony sale, which has been held here for more than three centuries. Smithfield became the city's principal cattle and horseflesh market in 1664, and probably takes its name in imitation of London's even longer-established Smithfield Market – an early example of either franchising or trademark theft!

Leave Smithfield by Friary Avenue, which is midway up on the right-hand side, and walk to the corner of Bow Street. Turn right, then after a few more paces turn left into the Old Jameson Distillery.

The Irish claim they invented whiskey (with an 'e') and John Jameson first started distilling here in the 1780s. Whiskey is no longer made on this site, but the guided tour takes you through the arcane processes of whiskey-making, from malting the grain to blending and ageing the final product. Naturally, there's a whiskey-tasting session at the end of each tour, which should fortify you for a trip (by lift) to the top of the 220ft (67m) distillery chimney. This has been transformed into a viewing tower from the top of which there is a breathtaking (and vertiginous) panoramic view over most of Dublin.

**OLD JAMESON DISTILLERY;**
www.jamesonwhiskey.com

## WHERE TO EAT

[O] **3RD STILL RESTAURANT,**
The Old Jameson Distillery,
Bow Street, Smithfield;
Tel: 807 2355.
An uncomplicated menu of traditional favourites makes this a good place to load up on calories before carrying on with your shopping. €

[O] **VAT HOUSE,**
6 Anglesea Street;
Tel: 671 5622.
Traditional pub with a good menu of bar snacks, such as soup, filled potato skins and baked potatoes, as well as more substantial meals including roasts, pasta, fish and chips and burgers. €

[O] **BEWLEY'S ORIENTAL CAFÉ,**
78–79 Grafton Street;
Tel: 677 6761.
Bewley's has been on the same site for more than 150 years, and still has an amiably old-fashioned air. It's a self-service café, with a fairly basic menu of sandwiches, soup, cakes, scones, teas and coffees. €

OPPOSITE: VIEW OVER DUBLIN FROM THE OLD JAMESON DISTILLERY CHIMNEY, SMITHFIELD

DISTANCE **2 miles (3.2km)**

ALLOW **3 hours**

START **North side of Father Mathew Bridge**

FINISH **Northwest corner of St Stephen's Green**

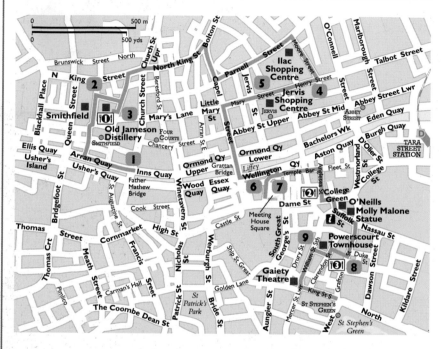

**3** Return to earth, leave the distillery, turn left and walk two blocks to the corner of King Street North, and turn right. After one block, cross Church Street and walk along King Street North for five short blocks, passing Berseford Street, Anne Street, Halston Street and Green Street to Capel Street. Turn right, then cross Capel Street, walk down to the corner of Parnell Street and turn left on to the south side of Parnell Street. Pass Wolfe Tone Street, Jervis Street and Chapel Lane on your right, carry on past the Ilac shopping complex, then turn right into Moore Street.

Like Smithfield, it seems that Moore Street has been supplying Dubliners with their everyday needs almost forever. However, while Smithfield dealt in livestock, Moore Street's stock-in-trade is an ever-widening array of fruit, flowers and vegetables. Had you visited this bustling, noisy market street even 20 years ago, you would have been lucky to find a vendor selling anything much

more exotic than a banana. How things have changed. Dublin's ethnic mix has widened dramatically and Dubliners have become much more cosmopolitan in their tastes. Now, as well as potatoes, turnips, apples and pears, you can pick up pineapples, mangoes, okra, aubergines and other comestibles from all over the world.

**4** At the foot of Moore Street, turn right into Henry Street.

This pedestrianized thoroughfare is liveliest in summer, when shoppers provide an audience for a handful of buskers and street performers, as well as targets for a number of scruffy panhandlers looking for a handout of spare change.

**5** At the end of Henry Street, continue straight on along Mary Street, passing between the two large modern shopping centres that straddle this small street, with the Jervis shopping centre on your left and the Ilac centre on your right. At the end of Mary Street, turn left on to Capel Street and walk south to the riverside. Cross Ormond Quay and walk straight on across Grattan Bridge. Cross Wellington Quay to the side opposite the Liffey, turn left, and after one short block turn right, then immediately left onto Temple Bar.

To your right, just after the corner of Temple Bar and Eustace Street, pedestrianized Cows Lane, despite its unpromising name, has become one of the smarter shopping streets in the rejuvenated Temple Bar district, with a concentration of very smart (and expensive) designer shops.

**6** Turn right and window-shop your way down Cows Lane – which is very short – to Meeting House Square.

On Saturdays the square is the venue for a weekly farmers' market, which sells a wide range of organic produce. There is an especially good choice of cheeses, so it's a good spot to stock up if you're planning a picnic.

**7** Leave Meeting House Square by way of Cows Lane to return to Temple Bar, and turn right. Walk along the south side of Temple Bar for three short blocks, and turn right on to Anglesea Street. At the south end of Anglesea Street, cross over Dame Street, turn left then almost immediately right on to the left-hand side of Suffolk Street. After a few yards, with O'Neill's pub on your left and the tourist information centre on the other side of the street, Suffolk Street takes a sharp kink to the left. Carry on to the end of this short block, and turn right on to Grafton Street.

Just before you cross over Suffolk Street to walk down Grafton Street, pause to pay your respects to Molly Malone, whose buxom bronze statue (affectionately known as 'The Tart with the Cart') stands on the corner, across from Trinity College. Remembered in the music-hall favourite song *Cockles and Mussels,* Molly Malone seems to have

been a real figure, with a reputation for selling sex as well as seafood, and who eventually succumbed to one of Dublin's frequent cholera epidemics, leaving a bereaved coterie of (male) admirers. Grafton Street is a lot smarter now than in Molly's day. It's where Dublin 'ladies who lunch' do their shopping in some of the capital's most expensive stores, including Brown Thomas, Dublin's very own answer to Harvey Nichols. Here you will find the usual hyper-expensive designer labels but also some of the best Irish bone china and crystal, in traditional and up-to-the-minute styles. Like the less up-market Henry Street, Grafton Street also has its regular contingent of buskers, beggars and street performers.

**8** Approximately halfway down Grafton Street turn right on to Johnson Court, a small side street. Follow this for one block to Clarendon Street. Cross to the opposite side, turn left then almost immediately right into Coppinger Row, then turn right again to enter Powerscourt Townhouse at the corner of Coppinger Row and William Street South.

This elegant shopping centre, with more than 40 shops, bars and restaurants including eight or more art galleries and antique dealers, is housed in an 18th-century Georgian mansion built for Richard Wingfield, 3rd Viscount Powerscourt (1730–88). Powerscourt was known as 'the French Earl' because of the dandified airs and graces he acquired while making the fashionable 'Grand Tour' of Europe's capitals.

**9** Walk to the foot of William Street South, turn left on Stephen Street, then follow King Street South, passing the Gaiety Theatre on your right, to the northwest corner of St Stephen's Green for buses back to the city centre.

131

FEINTS
STILL
2

# An Irish Pilgrimage to Glendalough

**The ruins of the monastic site founded by St Kevin at Glendalough in the 6th century occupy a lovely serene spot that richly rewards exploration.**

St Patrick, and the missionaries who came after him, brought Christianity to Ireland as early as the 5th century AD. St Kevin is said to have been of royal blood. A scion of the ruling dynasty of Leinster, born in AD498, he gave up the good life to become a hermit, a healer and a scholar – though in his time, scholarship amounted to little more than the painstaking copying and illustration of religious texts. His hermitage grew into a monastery, and after his death (*c*.618, at the age of 120) it became a major place of pilgrimage. His cult prospered, and his life was embroidered with legends. His saintly patience is exemplified by the story of the blackbird that perched on his outstretched hand to lay its egg while the saint was lost in prayer. Unwilling to disturb the nesting mother, St Kevin remained in the same position until the egg hatched. Like so many Christian holy places in Ireland, Glendalough was almost certainly a pagan sacred site until it was co-opted by Kevin and his disciples.

From the bus stop on the R756 road from Dublin, next to the car park on your left, walk up to the Glendalough Visitor Centre, easily found on the left just after you leave the car park.

Start your exploration of Glendalough with a visit to the centre's exhibition and multimedia show, which helps to place the site in its historical context. Most of Glendalough's buildings were built between the 8th and 12th centuries AD. All show the ravages of time, but some are in better shape than others, having been restored in the late 19th century. Like all Ireland's monasteries, Glendalough and its treasures attracted the unwelcome attention of Viking marauders from the late 9th century onwards, and it was repeatedly looted and pillaged. It gained a respite after the Dublin Vikings accepted Christianity in the 11th century, and after the Anglo-Norman conquest of Dublin it received some protection from the new English rulers. In 1398, however, it was partly destroyed by King Richard II's troops during one of Ireland's many rebellions against English rule. Glendalough's final downfall came with Henry VIII's dissolution of the monasteries of Ireland in 1539, but devout Catholics continued to make pilgrimages to St Kevin's shrine, as many do to this day.

**GLENDALOUGH VISITOR CENTRE;**

www.heritageireland.ie

2 From the visitor centre, take the road that forks left to the gatehouse to enter the site.

## WHERE TO EAT

🍽 GLENDALOUGH TAVERN,
Glendalough Hotel,
Glendalough, Bray, Co. Wicklow;
Tel: 0404 45135.
www.glendaloughhotel.com
Irish and international food served in a traditional pub atmosphere. €

🍽 WICKLOW HEATHER,
Laragh, Glendalough;
Tel: 0404 45157.
Irish breakfast is served all day. The lunch menu includes steaks and Irish beef stew, and for vegetarians, options such as broccoli and blue cheese bake. €€

This grey stone archway is the original entrance to the monastery precincts and is the only monastery gatehouse still standing in Ireland.

3 When you leave the gatehouse, walk south on the footpath for just less than 50yards (45m). Right in front of you stands Glendalough's largest single ruin, the slightly spooky-looking cathedral.

Now a roofless shell, the cathedral was built in the 12th century, not long after the Anglo-Norman conquest. In its churchyard, the small building known as the Priest's House was a mausoleum for higher-ranking monks and priests – among them, perhaps, St Kevin himself, for one of the three much-eroded figures carved above the door is said to be an

135

**DISTANCE 3 miles (5km)**

**ALLOW Half a day (journey time from Dublin 1 hour 15 minutes)**

**START Glendalough Visitor Centre (St Kevin's bus from Dublin, tel: 281 8119)**

**FINISH Glendalough Visitor Centre**

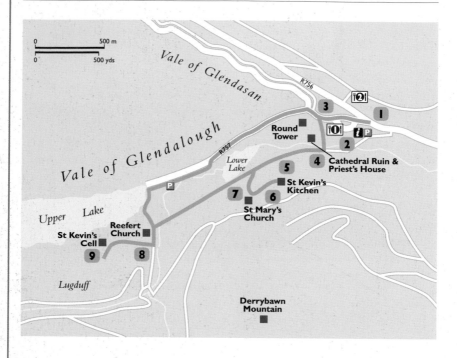

image of the saint accompanied by two of his acolytes. Between the Priest's House and the footpath is one of the finest of Glendalough's plethora of early stone crosses, carved from a single slab of granite and ornately decorated with intricate Celtic patterns.

**4** Turn right and head away from the footpath. Then walk west to Glendalough's most conspicuous landmark, the Round Tower, and the surrounding graveyard.

Just over 110ft (33m) tall, the slim, grey-stone tower, with just a few small windows, is one of the site's best-preserved buildings, having been restored during the 1870s.

**5** Continue to walk west and bear a little to your left for about half a mile (1km) to St Mary's Church.

This small church is one of the earliest buildings within the complex and is said to have been built some time around the

9th century AD. Walk around to the east side and look closely to detect much-worn traces of Romanesque stonework around the east window.

**6** Double-back eastwards along the north bank of the little River Glendassan, which flows through the pretty valley of Glendalough. In front of you and a little to your right you will see St Kevin's Kitchen.

So called because of its chimney-like belfry, this is not, of course, a kitchen at all but a pretty little oratory or prayer house, built entirely of grey local stone and dating from the 11th century (some 400 years after St Kevin's death).

**7** Returning to the footpath, turn right, cross the Glendassan by the footbridge, then turn right again and, with the stream and the Lower Lake on your right, walk for about 1,500yards (1.4km). Cross another small stream, and on your right, overlooking the Upper Lake, is Reefert Church.

Its name, derived from the Irish *Righ Fearta* (burial place of kings) indicates

LOWER LAKE, GLENDALOUGH

that this much–ruined church was probably built on or next to a graveyard of Irish monarchs, probably pre–dating the coming of Christianity.

**8** Carry on along the footpath to St Kevin's Cell, on your right.

Beehive-shaped structures like this much–ruined building are not uncommon in Ireland and are often said to have been the homes of hermits and holy men. In fact, they may well pre-date the Christian era by hundreds, if not thousands, of years, and like the *brochs* of

northern Scotland their original purpose remains a mystery to this day.

**9** Retrace your steps past Reefert Church and across the stream. On the other side the path divides. Turn left and walk around the east end of the Upper Lake, pausing to enjoy the view west along the narrow, mirror-calm water hemmed in between lush green hillsides. Next, cross the Glenealo stream that flows between the Upper and Lower Lakes. Follow the footpath to gain a vantage point across the Upper Lake.

Look south across the lake, which is less than 250yards (230m) wide, to spot two sites associated with St Kevin that are inaccessible on foot. On the lake shore stand the grey stone ruins of what is claimed to be St Kevin's very first church, Teampall-na-Skellig (church on the rock). Above it, and a little to the left, look for a shallow cave above a small ledge in the cliff. This may have been an ancient rock tomb, but legend has it that this was where St Kevin came to pray and to remove himself from worldly temptation. Temptation, however, pursued him, in the form of a nude and shapely woman; Kevin's response to her advances was to pitch her into the lake. To return to the beginning of this walk and transport back to Dublin, you can either retrace your steps along the footpath through the valley or leave the footpath where it joins the R757 road, just north of the footbridge over the Glenealo, and walk back along the road. This is marginally quicker, but less picturesque.

# The Dublin Riviera

**The coastline south from the estuary of the River Liffey is Dublin's own Riviera, complete with palm trees that flourish in the mild microclimate.**

Although it's technically a town in its own right, Dun Laoghaire (say 'Dun Leary'), seven miles (11km) south of the city centre, has been a favourite summer escape for Dubliners for at least two centuries. In a sycophantic outbreak of royal feeling, Dun Laoghaire was renamed Kingstown to honour the recently crowned George IV, who first set foot on Irish soil here in 1821. He was on a tour of the outlying provinces of the kingdom that he had finally inherited after a long spell as Prince Regent during the madness of his unfortunate father, George III. The Anglicized nomenclature stuck for exactly 100 years but after the Irish Free State was born, Dun Laoghaire reverted to its original name. Dublin, too, was officially renamed after the end of British rule, but with less success – Irish-language road signs and maps call it Baile Átha Cliath, but nobody else does. This is a walk for a sunny day, and in summer you might even go for a dip in what James Joyce called 'the snot-green, scrotum-tightening sea'.

Leave Dun Laoghaire DART station by the north exit facing the waterfront, and walk with the station on your right to the roundabout. On your left is the drably commercial Dun Laoghaire Harbour, Ireland's major ferry and freight port. Take the first turning on your right, Marine Road, crossing over the railway by a road bridge. Walk across the road and up the left-hand side for one block, past Moran Park and a dull modern shopping centre on your left, to George's Street Upper. Without crossing the street, turn left and walk two short blocks to Adelaide Street. Turn left here, walk to the end of the street and turn left to enter the National Maritime Museum.

The museum's key exhibits focus on the life of local hero Captain Robert Halpin, master of one of the world's first great steamships, the *Great Eastern*. Designed by the pioneering English engineer Isambard Kingdom Brunel, the ship was, in its day, at the leading edge of Victorian information technology. Under Halpin's command it laid the first telegraph cable across the Atlantic in 1866. Considering the newly invented technology available, this was some feat, and it heralded the dawn of a worldwide communications revolution. Suddenly, news travelled between Europe and America in minutes instead of days or weeks. Other exhibits include another piece of technology that was revolutionary in its day, the giant lens, rotated by clockwork, from the lighthouse on Howth Island, north of the Liffey.

2 Retrace your steps to George's Street Upper and turn left. Pass Mellifont Avenue on your left, then turn left onto Park Road and, with the small green space of People's Park on your right, walk towards the sea. At the end, cross the railway by the road bridge onto Queen's Road, cross over to the seaward side and turn right. On your left are the waters of Scotsman's Bay and ahead is the small headland of Sandycove and its small harbour. Continue down the esplanade for under half a mile (0.8km), along Marine Parade to Otranto

141

DISTANCE **2 miles (3.2km)**

ALLOW **2 hours (journey time from Dublin about 15 minutes)**

START **Dun Laoghaire DART station (trains from central Dublin stations)**

FINISH **Dalkey DART station**

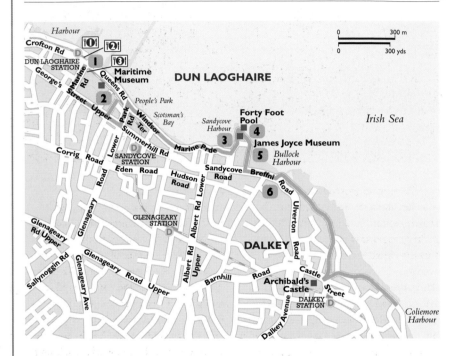

Place, and turn left, past a small park and a sea-bathing pool.

To your left is Sandycove's small harbour, where the working fishing boats are outnumbered by yachts and cruisers.

**3** Follow Sandycove Avenue round the harbour, with the harbour on your left, then follow it left over the headland above the village. When you reach the east side of the headland, look out for a flight of steps leading down to a small

bathing cove hemmed in by rocky slopes. This is Forty Foot Pool.

So called not because of its length, but because officers of the 40th Regiment of Foot, garrisoned here in the 19th century, used it as their private bathing spot, where they enjoyed swimming naked. It continued to be an all-male nude bathing preserve long after the 40th left for England, but is now open to women as well, if they are brave enough to face the chilly water of the Irish Sea.

4 Turn right, with the sea on your left, and after a few yards turn right to enter the squat, decidedly military-looking round stone building that overlooks the sea.

The James Joyce Museum is housed in one of a string of miniature fortresses, known as Martello towers, which were built along the Dublin Bay Coast in 1804 against the threat of a French invasion. With the end of the Napoleonic Wars, these little forts became redundant, and some were converted into homes. A century later, one of the tenants was the poet, author and friend of James Joyce, Oliver St John Gogarty, who rented this tower for the princely sum of £8 a year. In September 1904 Gogarty invited Joyce to spend a week with him here, and the experience inspired Joyce to set the opening chapter of *Ulysses* here and to fictionalize his host as one of the book's chief characters: 'stately, plump

Buck Mulligan'. In 1962 the round tower, which is just 40ft (12m) high, was turned into a museum dedicated to Joyce's literary career, and within is an eclectic collection of his possessions, including Joyce's guitar, one of his ties, his wallet, walking stick and the cabin trunk which accompanied him into self-imposed literary exile in Italy, France and Switzerland. On its shelves are rare first editions of Joyce's works, including a unique edition of *Ulysses* illustrated by the French artist Henri Matisse.

**JAMES JOYCE MUSEUM;**

www.visitdublin.com

5 Leaving the tower, return to Sandycove Avenue and continue, with the sea on your left, to a right-angle bend. With the sea at your back, continue back to Sandycove Road. Turn left, and follow the road along the coast for approximately a mile (1.6km) until you reach Dalkey.

143

ABOVE: ARCHBOLD'S CASTLE, DALKEY VILLAGE

This small seaside town, which was the setting for Flann O'Brien's surreal novel *The Dalkey Archives*, has long been a sought-after residential area, and the stylish 19th-century villas that line its winding streets command high prices. Palm trees and other subtropical plants growing in many gardens give it a distinctly Mediterranean atmosphere (at least on a sunny day). Dalkey was nicknamed the 'Town of Seven Castles' because of the fortified tower-houses built by Anglo-Irish families during the turbulent times of the 15th and 16th centuries, when Ireland's rulers had perpetually to be on guard against attacks by Irish rebels and their Spanish allies. One of the surviving towers, now known as Archbold's Castle, can be seen on the corner of Dalkey Main Street, just south of Dalkey sports ground.

6 From the town centre, turn left to walk downhill on Harbour Road to Dalkey's Coliemore Harbour.

Clearly visible less than a mile (1.6km) offshore is Dalkey Island. The island is a seabird sanctuary where the only signs of former human habitation are a Martello tower and the shell of a medieval Benedictine chapel. In the 9th and 10th centuries the island was a Viking lair, and in the 18th century it was the venue for an annual crowning of the make-believe 'King of Dalkey' and his mock-parliament by a group of Dubliners. By the time of the French Revolution in the late 18th century, this ceremony, originally carried out just for

laughs, had acquired political overtones which worried the authorities, and in 1797 – just a year before the French-backed rising of the United Irishmen, led by Wolfe Tone – it was banned, only to be revived as an annual fun event in the late 1970s. In summer boat trips are available to Dalkey Island. Retrace your steps to the centre of Dalkey and the DART station (which is clearly signposted) to return to Dublin.

## WHERE TO EAT

🍴 HARTLEY'S,
1 Harbour Road, Dun Laoghaire;
Tel: 280 6767.
The emphasis is on seafood, with a different mussel dish every day. Also meat, salad and pasta options. Popular so booking is advised. €€

🍴 PURPLE OCEAN,
St Michael's Pier, Dun Laoghaire;
Tel: 284 5590.
www.purpleocean.ie
Quayside restaurant that serves an eclectic mix of dishes ranging from deep fried brie and salmon fishcakes to Thai curries and mushroom and coriander stroganoff. €€

🍴 CAFÉ MAO,
The Pavilion, Dun Laoghaire;
Tel: 214 8090.
www.cafemao.com
Overlooking the sea, Café Mao has an excellent array of wok-cooked, Asian influenced dishes. €€

DALKEY ISLAND SEEN FROM COLIEMORE HARBOUR

# Saints and Sinners: Around Rathfarnham

**Rathfarnham village is associated with an array of events, anecdotes and prominent Dublin figures, some of which are portrayed in this walk.**

Padraig Pearse, one of the leading firebrands of the Republican movement and a key figure in the Easter Rising of 1916, William Connolly, founder member of Dublin's infamous Hell-Fire Club, and Mother Teresa of Calcutta are just three of the more famous folk to be associated with Rathfarnham, but the castle and the village have other stories to tell. During the 18th century, Rathfarnham became a popular address for the Irish gentry, many of whom built country homes around the village, and at the same time the water of the River Dodder was harnessed to drive paper mills and textile mills. Rathfarnham's brief industrial era came to an end in the 19th century, when steam power supplanted water-power, and the village then became little more than a dormitory suburb of Dublin. But Rathfarnham's history has not always been peaceful. The Yellow House Tavern stands on the site of an earlier hostelry, whose landlord, Michael Eades, sheltered members of the United Irishmen movement on the run after the failure of their rising in 1798; in 1804 it was sacked in reprisal by British soldiers and militiamen.

1 From the corner of Main Street and Rathfarnham Road, walk south, passing on your way a small red and white building that is now the home of the Rathfarnham Athletic Club.

This is Rathfarnham's Old Courthouse. Built in 1913, it would no doubt have been viewed with disfavour as a symbol of British rule by Padraig Pearse, the fervent Irish nationalist whose school for boys stood not far away, in St Enda's Park.

2 Continue down Main Street. Do not turn left on Rathfarnham Gate, which, confusingly, no longer leads to the castle since a bypass road was built in 1979 between the castle and the village. At the foot of Main Street, turn left onto Butterfield Avenue.

Thomas Addis Emmet (1764–1827), a prominent figure in the United Irishmen movement and elder brother of Robert Emmet, leader of the abortive rising of 1803, is said to have lived nearby before the rising. When it broke out, however, he was in Paris, trying to wheedle troops and weapons from Napoleon Bonaparte. The rising failed, Robert Emmet was hanged and buried in a secret grave (it has never been located) and Thomas left for America, where he became a successful lawyer and attorney general of New York state.

3 Turn left again, cross Rathfarnham Road and enter Rathfarnham Castle, which stands just north of the corner of Rathfarnham Road and Grange Road.

## WHERE TO EAT

🍴 YELLOW HOUSE,
1 Willbrook Road;
Tel: 493 2994.
Rathfarnham's historic landmark tavern serves light meals in the bar and more formal evening meals and Sunday lunches in the restaurant upstairs. €€

🍴 REEVES RESTAURANT,
Eden Pub, Grange Road;
Tel: 495 6677.
Every kind of chicken from Tex-Mex to Cajun to Chinese, plus steaks, a small choice of vegetarian dishes, and a big choice of starters. €€

In front of you is a sturdy, white-painted building that looks part mansion, part fortress. Rathfarnham Castle was built around 1583 for Adam Loftus, the Yorkshireman who became Anglican Archbishop of Dublin and Lord Chancellor of Ireland. With Spain supporting Irish lords in rebellion against English rule, Loftus clearly felt the need for a home that could be easily defended. He took out an extra insurance policy too: secret tunnels led from the castle cellars to exits in what is now Rathfarnham Golf Club's Castle Course, and to the village churchyard, so that if the defences failed the castle's inmates still had a chance to escape. Sadly, both tunnels are now bricked up. At the outbreak of the English Civil War, Rathfarnham was besieged by

149

OPPOSITE: A STONE LION STATUE, RATHFARNHAM CASTLE

DISTANCE  1.5 miles (2.4km)

ALLOW  2 hours (journey from Dublin about 15 minutes)

START  Main Street, Rathfarnham (bus 16 or 16A from Dublin)

FINISH  St Enda's Park, Rathfarnham

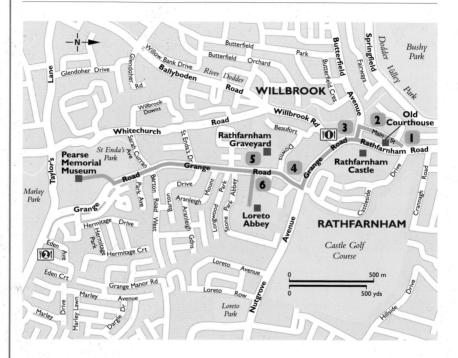

Irish rebels in 1641 and garrisoned by English Parliamentary troops in the following year, when the Parliamentarian leader Oliver Cromwell is said to have stayed here before sending his troops to carry out the notorious massacres of Irish soldiers and civilians at Wexford and Drogheda. The castle remained in Loftus hands until 1724, when a dissolute descendant, Philip, Earl of Wharton, sold it to pay his debts. The buyer was the Right Honourable William Connolly, MP, Speaker of the House of Commons

– and a founder member of the notorious Hell-Fire Club. Legend has it that this group of rakes, drunks and 'bucks' would meet at the hunting lodge that Connolly had built in the Dublin Mountains above Rathfarnham to drink, debauch, and hold black Masses to summon up the Devil. There doesn't seem to be much truth in this – the Hell-Fire Club did exist, and Connolly was associated with it, but its members seem to have done most of their misbehaving in the Eagle Tavern on Cork Hill, beside Dublin

OPPOSITE: LORETO ABBEY

Castle. But one gruesome find hints at skulduggery at Rathfarnham too. In 1880 builders discovered the skeleton of a young woman in a hidden chamber in the hollow walls of the building's first floor. An inquest determined that the cadaver had been there for more than 130 years. Legend has it that she was locked into the secret room while two rivals fought a duel for her hand in marriage. The survivor was to release her; unfortunately, they killed each other and she was left to die of hunger and thirst. In 1912, property developers Bailey and Gibson bought the castle and built houses over most of the grounds and turned the remaining open space into a golf course. Delaware Properties, which bought the property in 1985, planned to demolish it but after a public campaign it was acquired by Heritage Ireland, which is gradually restoring different sections. Inside, the most striking parts are the finely proportioned rooms and halls designed by two great Scottish architects, Sir William Chambers and James 'Athenian' Stuart.

**RATHFARNHAM CASTLE;**

www.heritageireland.ie

**4** At the junction with Nutgrove Avenue, Grange Road turns sharply to the right. Follow it past the corner of Beaufort Downs, on your right, then turn right into Rathfarnham graveyard.

Near the entrance to the graveyard, to your left, is the tomb of yet another noted rebel, Captain James Kelly. Nicknamed 'the Knight of Glendoo',

Kelly was a local leader of the Fenian Rising of 1867. The Fenians, like so many Irish rebel movements, hoped to trigger a general insurrection all over Ireland (and overseas – they even tried to invade Canada from the US) but were quickly quelled. Captain Kelly, however, escaped serious British retribution and lived until his 70th year, dying in 1915.

**5** Go back to Grange Road, cross over, and enter the grounds of Loreto Abbey.

Originally called Rathfarnham House, this massive Georgian pile was built in 1725 for William Palliser, a wealthy Yorkshireman who made his fortune in the arms industry before moving to Ireland to built a palatial home, where he entertained guests including Handel, Jonathan Swift and the poet Thomas Moore. There's a story that at one soirée the guests locked Moore in one of the rooms and refused to let him out until he had composed a lyrical piece for them. The result was his most famous air, *Oft in the Stilly Night*. In 1821 the Catholic archbishop of Dublin, Dr Daniel Murray, bought the house in order to set up a religious school for girls. It eventually spawned 22 daughter-convents as far afield as Australia, Africa and Mauritius. Its most famous pupil is Mother Teresa of Calcutta (1910–97), who enrolled here in 1928 at the age of 18, taking the name of Loreto's first Mother Superior. Loreto finally closed in 1999. The historic building is now part of a luxury apartment complex.

6 Return to Grange Road, turn left and then walk south. After passing Barton Drive and Barton Road West on your left, cross to the west side of Grange Road and enter St Enda's Park. Walk south to the Pearse Memorial Museum, housed in a sturdy grey stone building with a four-columned Doric portico, in the centre of the park.

Padraig Pearse (1879–1916) set up St Enda's School for Boys here in 1908 to educate boys in the Irish language. A fervent nationalist, Pearse believed the national language – which was rapidly dying out by the early 20th century – was essential to building a national identity. In 1913 he became a member of the secret, radical Irish Republican Brotherhood and was soon one of its leaders. He seems to have had a bloodthirsty, mystical streak; writing about the battles of World War I in 1915, he spoke of 'the old heart of the earth' needing to 'be warmed with the red wine of the battlefields'. Blood sacrifice in the nationalist cause is a common theme of his speeches and writings, and it was this that led him to march the 5 miles (8km) from Rathfarnham to the General Post Office in Dublin to proclaim the Irish Republic on 24 April 1916, beginning the Easter Rising. Six days later, Pearse and his comrades surrendered to the British. On 3 May, after a summary court martial, he and 14 others, including his younger brother Willie, were executed in Kilmainham Gaol. Inside the former schoolhouse, a 20-minute audiovisual show, *This Man Kept a School*, tells his story. When you are ready to return to central Dublin, walk back to Rathfarnham Main Street and take bus 16 or 16A.

ABOVE: THE PEARSE MUSEUM IN ST EDNA'S PARK

# Vintage Cars and Radio Stars

**Set on a headland overlooking Dublin Bay, Howth is a pretty coastal town with steeply sloping streets leading to a former fishing harbour.**

Howth's fishing fleet has dwindled and in its spacious harbour crab and lobster boats are now outnumbered by enviable sailing yachts and leisure craft. Set just to the east of the narrow isthmus that links Howth Head with the mainland, and facing north across the Irish Sea, Howth attracted the attention of early seafarers and was a significant Norse settlement from the 9th to the 11th centuries. An early Christian king of Dublin endowed its first abbey, and the descendants of a dynasty of Anglo-Normans still live in the castle built by their ancestors during the 14th century. Hydrangeas, rhododendrons and azaleas flourish in the grounds of Howth Castle, and in public parks and the private gardens of cottages and villas. With its sea views and pretty surroundings, Howth has some of the most expensive real estate in the area. As a result, unfortunately, property developers have overbuilt much of the peninsula, and the suburban sprawl that surrounds the original harbour village is a bit uninspiring.

From Howth station turn right on to Harbour Road. Continue west to Howth Road, with the station on your right. Cross over to the churchyard, and just west of the church turn left into the grounds of Howth Castle (also known as Howth Demesne) and follow the footpath towards the castle. Just before reaching the castle, the footpath takes a right-angle turn to the right. Follow it till you reach a right turn for the National Transport Museum, clearly signposted.

In 1949 a small group of transport enthusiasts made an unsuccessful bid to rescue three of Dublin's last remaining tramcars from the breaker's yard. They failed, but the National Transport Museum, run entirely by volunteers, grew from that attempt. Its collection now comprises more than 100 classic buses, trams, lorries, cars, fire engines and ambulances. The oldest vehicle in the collection, a horse-drawn Merriweather fire appliance, was built in 1883. In 1948 it was placed in storage in a disused distillery and forgotten about until 1996, when it was rediscovered, given to the museum, and found to be in remarkably good working order.

## NATIONAL TRANSPORT MUSEUM OF IRELAND;

www.nationaltransportmuseum.org

Turn about and retrace your steps with Howth Castle on your right. The castle grounds are most attractive in May and June, when the colourful azaleas are in full bloom.

Although partly in ruins, the ancestral home of the St Lawrence family, Earls and Barons of Howth, is still lived in by descendants of the 1st Baron. The first castle was built here in the 14th century, but in the late 19th century Sir Edward

155

DISTANCE **1.5 miles (2.4km)**

ALLOW **2 hours (journey time from Dublin about 20 minutes)**

START **Howth DART Station (trains from central Dublin DART stations)**

FINISH **Howth DART Station**

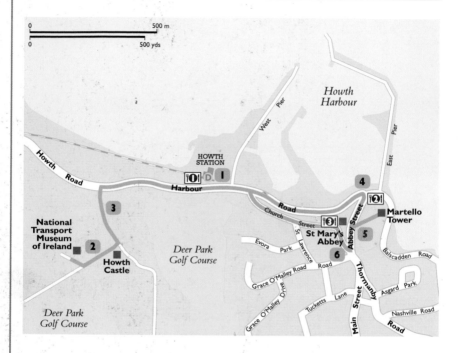

Lutyens was commissioned to build a virtually new stately home on the site. In 1576, the famous female pirate Grace O'Malley made an impromptu visit to the 8th Baron, only to be informed that he was at dinner and she couldn't come in. Peeved, she kidnapped the baron's grandson (later the 10th Baron) and held him hostage until the baron pledged that the castle's gates would forever be kept open to unexpected guests and an empty place would be set at each meal. The baron's descendants, the Gaisford-St

Lawrence family, apparently still keep this promise, but it would probably not be acceptable to stroll in and demand a free dinner. The castle isn't open to the public.

**3** Retrace your steps to Howth station and follow the harbour promenade to the corner of Harbour Road and Abbey Street, with Howth Harbour on your left.

The pretty harbour was formerly home to a large fleet of fishing smacks, but

OPPOSITE: HOWTH HARBOUR LIGHTHOUSE

marine pollution, the massive over-fishing of the Irish Sea by Spanish and French trawlers, along with limits imposed by the European Union on how much can be caught, have virtually destroyed the local fishing industry and only a few crab and lobster boats share Howth Harbour with the numerous yachts and motor cruisers.

**4** Cross Abbey Street and turn right down it. On your left (opposite the Abbey Tavern), you will see a squat, circular tower. Turn left to enter it.

This is one of a chain of Martello towers built around 1804 along the coasts of Ireland, England and the Channel Islands to deter a French invasion of Britain and Ireland. Their name comes from a small medieval fortress on Cape Mortella on the French island of Corsica (ironically, the birthplace of Napoleon Bonaparte, the very man whose invasion plans they were intended to thwart). Somehow, Mortella was mis-transcribed as Martello and the name stuck. In 1805, soon after the towers were completed, the combined French and Spanish fleets were destroyed at the Battle of Trafalgar, the threat of a French invasion vanished, and the towers became redundant. In the 1840s this one was used as a telegraph cable station. On 25 November 1903 the American inventor Lee de Forest sent the first wireless radio messages from here to Holyhead in Wales, an achievement that was later overshadowed by the more famous Guglielmo Marconi, who

THE MARTELLO TOWER HOUSING YE OLDE HURDY GURDY MUSEUM

also broadcast radio messages from this spot; Marconi seems to have been both a more adept self-publicist and more commercially minded than poor de Forest. Appropriately, the tower is now home to Ye Olde Hurdy Gurdy Museum of Vintage Radio, which houses hundreds of early radios, wind-up gramophones, Morse code transmitters and lots of other arcane pieces of broadcasting and communications equipment. In the era of the mobile phone, the Blackberry® and the MP3 player, they look incredibly clunky – a reminder of how breathtakingly quickly technology has progressed in little more than a century.
**YE OLDE HURDY GURDY MUSEUM;**
http://ei5em.110mb.com/museum.html

**5** Retrace your steps, cross Abbey Street and turn left, passing the post office on your right, to the junction of Church Street, which forms a V.

Between the two streets are the ruins and churchyard of St Mary's Abbey, which was founded in 1042 by Sidric, or Sigtrygg, the Viking King of Dublin. Little or nothing remains of the original 11th-century building, and the roofless walls of the abbey date mostly from the 15th and 16th centuries. Like other monasteries and abbeys in Ireland and England, it fell into ruin and disuse after Henry VIII's dissolution of the monasteries in the second half of the 16th century. The abbey ruins are not open to the public, but in the churchyard you can see the tomb of Christopher St Lawrence, 8th Baron Howth (whose

## WHERE TO EAT

🍴 THE BLOODY STREAM,
14 West Pier;
Tel: 839 5076.
This restaurant and bar overlooking Howth Harbour has super views and an affordable menu of steaks, salads and seafood. €€

🍴 KING SITRIC FISH RESTAURANT,
East Pier;
Tel: 832 5235.
Not cheap, but probably the best restaurant and seafood bar in Howth, with superb fresh crab and lobster for those in an extravagant mood. €€€

🍴 ABBEY TAVERN,
Abbey Street;
Tel: 839 0307.
Authentic 16th-century tavern with flagstone floors, thick stone walls, peat fires and even gaslight. Renowned for its seafood. €€

grandson was kidnapped by the pirate Grace O'Malley) and his wife Elizabeth.

**6** Turn right up Church Street to return to Harbour Road and walk back to Howth DART station for trains to Dublin. If you are feeling energetic, follow the Dublin Coast Trail, which starts at Balscadden Road opposite the Martello tower, along the cliffs back to the city (about four hours' walking).

A VIEW OVER HOWTH HARBOUR

# From Jameson Distillery to Kilmainham

**Irish whiskey and Irish stout are world famous, and the prowess of Ireland's fighting men is the stuff of legends.**

The water of the River Liffey has been a key ingredient in two of Dublin's most famous beverages for centuries, and this walk starts with a taste of the 'dew of the barley' then follows the Liffey to Kilmainham, a spot forever associated with the dark taste of Guinness stout and the dark days that followed the defeat of the Easter Rising of 1916. It also includes two very different museums of the arts, one of which looks back to the roots of Ireland's earliest traditions of the decorative arts, while the other displays works of art in a much more modern tradition. One of the top stops along this route is the Guinness Storehouse®, rated Ireland's number one visitor attraction. To avoid having to queue here, book your ticket in advance at www.guinness-storehouse.com (this also gives you a 10 per cent discount). On a sunny day, you can link this walk with Walk 8 for a longer day out, including a stroll around Phoenix Park.

From North King Street North, turn south and walk down the right-hand side of Bow Street. There is an easy-to-see landmark ahead of you – the former chimney of the Jameson whiskey distillery. After passing two small side streets – Brown Street, then Friary Avenue – on your right, turn right into the Old Jameson Distillery.

Whiskey is no longer made here, but visitors are given a free glass at the end of the tour, and the distillery also offers tasting sessions during which you can sample the various styles of whiskey made by Ireland's best-known distillers. The guided tour explains the intricacies and history of whiskey-making, which the Irish claim to have invented. Knowledge of the distilling process seems to have been brought to Ireland from the Islamic world by monks, who learned the skill from the Muslims who invented it. In the Middle East and North Africa, the process was used to distil essential oils from flowers, fruit and nuts to make perfumes and incense, but the Irish seem to have been the first to use it to make a potent drink. Jameson's began distilling here in the 1780s, and the tour shows you some of the traditional whiskey-making equipment, including copper stills and the oak casks in which whiskey is matured.

**OLD JAMESON DISTILLERY;**

www.jamesonwhiskey.com

**2** Leaving the distillery, turn right on New Church Street to reach Smithfield, the site of Dublin's former meat and livestock market.

## WHERE TO EAT

🍽 GRAVITY®BAR,
Guinness Storehouse®,
St James's Gate;
Tel: 408 4800.
This circular, glass-sided bar on the roof of the Guinness Storehouse® offers a free pint at the end of your brewery tour and also serves bar meals. It also has panoramic views of the city. €€

🍽 GRASS ROOTS CAFÉ,
Irish Museum of Modern Art,
Military Road;
Tel: 612 9900.
The Museum of Modern Art's bright modern café sells hot and cold drinks, snacks, salads, sandwiches, cakes and pastries. €

The cobbled rectangle opened in 1664 as a cattle and horse market (like its namesake in London). In the early 21st century, however, it has seen remarkable gentrification and is now a mix of up-market houses and apartments, shops, studios and galleries, which is barely recognizable as the Smithfield of yesteryear. A horse market is still held at Smithfield but there is mounting pressure for the market to be moved or closed altogether. In 1964, Smithfield stood in for locations in Eastern Europe during the filming of John le Carré's film *The Spy Who Came in from the Cold*. The 220ft (67m) distillery chimney, now converted into a viewing tower, is a prominent

163

DISTANCE **2 miles (3.2km)**

ALLOW **3 hours**

START **Corner of King Street North and Bow Street**

FINISH **Kilmainham Gaol, Inchicore Road**

landmark here. At the time of writing it was closed for maintenance, but when it does re-open it offers outstanding views.

**3** Leave Smithfield from its south end and walk down short, narrow Arran Street to Arran Quay, on the north bank of the Liffey. Do not cross over, but turn right and walk along the quays (first Arran Quay, then Ellis Quay) with the river on your left, passing Mellowes Bridge on your left. Just before the end of Ellis Key, with Rory O'More Bridge ahead of you, cross Blackhall Place then turn immediately left into Benburb Street. The entrance to the National Museum of Ireland's Decorative Arts and History Section is one short block up,

on your right, on the north side of Benburb Street at Collins Barracks.

This former military building (renamed, following independence, in memory of Michael Collins, commander of the Irish Free State forces during the Civil War) has been converted into an outstanding museum. The collection traces Ireland's social and cultural history through the centuries, and includes silver, glass and pottery, furniture and folk costumes. It also features a new exhibition of military history, 'Soldiers and Chiefs: The Irish at War at Home and Abroad, 1550–2001', outlining how war and resistance have shaped Ireland's culture. Irish noblemen and their followers served as soldiers

ARRAN QUAY

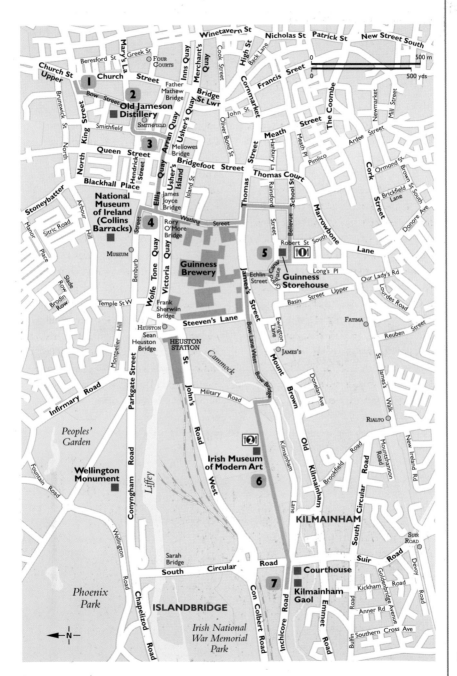

of fortune in the armies of England's enemies, France and Spain, from the mid-16th century and made common cause with Scottish Jacobites against William of Orange in the strife of 1688–90 and the Scottish risings of 1715 and 1745. A descendant of one of these 'Wild Geese', Macmahon, even became a Marshal of France and President of the French Republic. But Irishmen also served their English masters loyally in the battles of the Napoleonic Wars, the Crimean War, Britain's colonial wars, and World War I. After independence, although Ireland remained firmly neutral, many Irish volunteers fought in the British Army during World War II, and Irish soldiers have also served with distinction as members of UN peacekeeping forces in many conflicts around the world.

**NATIONAL MUSEUM OF IRELAND;**
www.museum.ie

**4** Retrace your steps to the Liffey, cross Rory O'More Bridge and walk south on the left-hand side of Watling Street. The Guinness Brewery occupies a vast site stretching from Victoria Quay on the south side of the Liffey to James's Street. At the foot of Watling Street, cross Thomas Street, turn left and then right into Crane Street. Walk down, cross Rainsford Street, then turn right onto Bellevue, then Market Street to the Guinness Storehouse®. This seven-storey building is conspicuous because of the glass-sided Gravity®Bar like a flying saucer that surmounts it.

Arthur Guinness began making the black brew that is Ireland's most famous drink here at St James's Gate in 1759. Guinness is now exported all over the world in kegs, cans and bottles and is also brewed in several other countries, including the UK. In West Africa, it has a reputation as a libido enhancer; in Malaysia it is regarded as a healthful elixir; and as recently as the 1970s some British hospitals gave recuperating patients a bottle a day to aid their recovery. But as any Dubliner will tell you, unless it's made in Dublin from true Liffey water, it's not the real thing. A visit to the

Guinness Storehouse®, housed in a sturdy red-brick building which was originally one the brewery's fermentation houses, will make you an instant expert.

**GUINNESS STOREHOUSE®;**

www.guinness-storehouse.com

5 Leave the brewery, turn right and follow Market Street to Grand Canal Place, which is shaped like an inverted horseshoe. Follow it as it curves to your left, then turn right on to Echlin Street, take the first left on to James's Street, and walk west. Take Bow Lane West, which forks off James's Street to the right. Follow this as far as Bow Bridge, then almost immediately turn right on to Irwin Street. This short street leads you to Military Road. Cross this to enter the Irish Museum of Modern Art.

The museum's home is a gracious 17th-century building with a green copper spire, set in formal gardens. This was the Royal Hospital, designed in 1680 by Sir William Robinson and strongly influenced by the architecture of Les Invalides in Paris. Like Les Invalides, it was built as a hospice for wounded or crippled soldiers. Its classical interior now houses a growing collection of challenging contemporary art and provides a venue for visiting exhibitions.

**IRISH MUSEUM OF MODERN ART;**

www.imma.ie

6 Walk west through the grounds of the museum to the South Circular Road, cross over and enter Inchicore Road. Pass the courthouse on the corner on your left, then turn left into Kilmainham Gaol.

This huge prison holds an iconic place in Irish history. Between its opening in 1796 and its closure as a jail in 1924, many of the leaders of the Irish independence movement did time here, among them Robert Emmet, Charles Stewart Parnell and Eamon de Valera. Some – such as Pearse, Connolly and the other leaders of the Easter Rising – were executed here.

7 Buses 51B, 51C, 78A, 79 or 79A take you back to the city centre, but to link this itinerary with Walk 8, walk up South Circular Road, cross the river by Sarah Bridge, cross Conyngham Road, turn left, then turn right to enter Phoenix Park by the Islandbridge Gate. Turn right and follow Wellington Road to the Wellington Monument.

167

# On the Waterfront

**This stroll along the waterfront reveals a rich vein of hidden history beneath the 21st-century veneer of Dublin's rejuvenated docklands.**

Dublin's docklands were in decline through much of the 20th century, and it wasn't until the 1990s that Ireland's much-vaunted 'Celtic Tiger' economy began to breathe new life into the moribund areas either side of the lower Liffey. Completion of the Irish Financial Services Centre (IFSC), a new precinct of offices, shops, restaurants and apartments, heralded the region's rebirth. The IFSC, like London's Docklands, is creating a city within a city, and is a melange of restored historic buildings – such as the chq building, a 19th-century warehouse, which has become a chic shopping centre – and gleaming 21st-century towers. Two of these are likely to be under construction when you visit. The U2 Tower, south of the river, and the Point Tower, next to the Point Village at the east end of North Wall Quay, will each be 390ft (120m) in height and will become the keynote landmarks of the new Dublin docklands. In many ways, this is a walk through history in the making: be prepared for short diversions from the exact route described here because of ongoing construction work.

1 Leave Connolly Station by the Amiens Street exit and turn left on Amiens Street. Walk down this busy and unappealing street to Memorial Road, and, with the lawns of the Custom House on your right, continue down this very short road to Custom House Quay and the Liffey. Cross to the riverside of the quay and turn around to face the Custom House. To your left is the Famine Memorial.

This group of rather abstract bronze figures commemorates all those who died and were forced to leave Ireland during the Great Famine of 1845–48, when the Irish potato crop was destroyed by blight, depriving many people of their main, if not only, source of food. It is estimated that up to one million people starved to death. Many more died aboard the vessels that came to be known as 'coffin ships' on the way to America, where they hoped to begin a new life. Many of the luckier ones settled in the slums of the Dublin docklands, giving the area, and the city, a new character and bringing with them an abiding resentment of the British ruling class, who did too little, too late, to prevent the famine. Take a quick look at the grand Georgian front of the Custom House (see Walk 7) with its green copper dome crowned by an allegorical figure representing Commerce.

2 Continue walking east along Custom House Quay, crossing over the entrance to George's Dock on the left-hand side.

## WHERE TO EAT

🍴 **THE VAULTS,**
Connolly Station, Amiens Street;
Tel: 605 4700.
Housed in the echoing brick vaults underneath Connolly Station, with a menu that stretches from soup and fish and chips to Caesar salad, tandoori chicken, crispy duck won ton and salmon linguine. €€

🍴 **ELY CHQ,**
chq, Custom House Quay;
Tel: 672 0010.
www.elywinebar.ie
Trendy new wine bar at the chq complex with a choice of breakfast, all-day and canapé menu, brunch and a more expensive set lunch and dinner. €€/€€€

🍴 **D-ONE,**
IFSC, North Wall Quay;
Tel: 856 1622.
Overlooking the Liffey, this new restaurant offers traditional Irish dishes such as roast chicken and fish and chips with a modern twist. It's a favourite with IFSC inmates at lunchtime, so booking is advised. €€€

The Abbey Theatre, Ireland's national theatre, is scheduled to move to a new home beside St George's Dock from its original site at 26 Abbey Street. The Abbey was the dramatic launch pad for the careers of most of the leading Irish

169

**DISTANCE** I mile (1.6km)

**ALLOW** 1–2 hours

**START** Connolly Station (Amiens Street exit)

**FINISH** Grand Canal Dock DART station

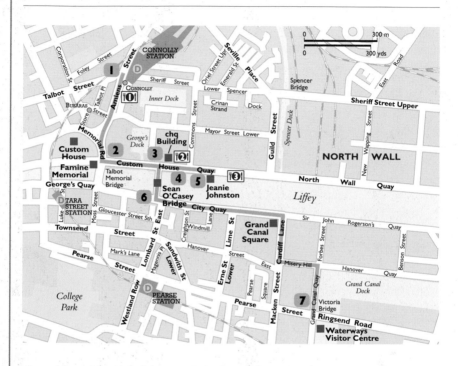

playwrights of the 20th century, including one of the North Wall district's most famous sons, Sean O'Casey (see Walk 12).

**3** Immediately after passing the entrance of George's Dock, turn left and you are facing the east front of a conspicuous and immaculately restored brick warehouse block.

This is the chq building, formerly a wine and tobacco warehouse built in 1820 and for most of its life known simply as Stack A. In 1856 it was famously the venue for the Crimean War Banquet, held to celebrate the return of 3,000 Irish soldiers from the war in the Crimea between Britain (in alliance with Turkey and France) and Russia. In the early 21st century it was splendidly restored and converted into a smart shopping centre. Go in only if you want to add to your collection of expensive designer wear and yuppie accessories.

**CHQ BUILDING;**

www.chq.ie

OPPOSITE: A REPLICA OF THE SAILING SHIP *JEANIE JOHNSTON*

**4** Return to Custom House Quay, cross to the riverside, and continue east along the Liffey. Just after passing Commons Street, you should see the three masts of a traditional sailing ship.

The barque *Jeanie Johnston*, of which this is a painstaking copy, was built in Quebec in 1847 and sold to the Tralee merchant Nicholas Donovan. She carried timber from Canada and America to Ireland, and emigrants from Ireland to America. Unlike many of the ships that carried people fleeing poverty and famine across the Atlantic, the *Jeanie Johnston* was not a 'coffin ship' – she carried 2,500 people on 16 voyages with not a single death, mainly due to the care taken by her owner, her captain and her ship's doctor. Supplies provided for each passenger comprised 21 quarts of water, 2.5lb bread or biscuit, 1lb flour, 5lb oatmeal, 2lb rice, 2oz tea, 8oz sugar and 8oz molasses. These rations had to last for up to eight weeks. The on-board museum, with its life-size figures, gives you a realistic glimpse of the cramped and spartan life in the emigrant berths; fortunately no attempt is made to recreate the stench of a ship that lacked even rudimentary toilets and washing facilities. The replica ship was built during the 1990s and funded by the people of Tralee and County Kerry as a memorial to the victims and survivors of the famine. Since then, the *Jeanie Johnston* has sailed across the Atlantic and all over Europe. She is used as a sail training ship as well as a floating museum.

**JEANIE JOHNSTON;**

www.jeaniejohnston.ie

**5** Walk back along the riverside to one of the Liffey's newest landmarks, the Sean O'Casey Bridge, which is in plain view ahead of you. Turn to the left and walk across it.

Designed by architect Cyril O'Neill and named in honour of one of Dublin's great dramatic and political radicals, the bridge, built in 2005, is a dramatic structure in its own right. With a span of almost 325ft (100m), its angular steel walkway is supported by two granite piers and splits into two sections, which can be raised through 90 degrees to allow vessels to pass.

**6** Turn left at the end of the bridge and walk along City Quay, then Sir John Rogerson's Quay, with the Liffey on your left, for four blocks and turn right on to Cardiff Lane. Take the first left, Misery Hill, then turn right and walk down Grand Canal Quay, with Grand Canal Dock on your left. To your left, MacMahon Bridge crosses the water of Grand Canal Dock to Ringsend Road.

Until the building of the Grand Canal Dock, Ringsend, at the mouth of the River Dodder, which flows into the Liffey just east of the dock, was a small fishing and trading port and the setting for a maritime mystery yarn. In 1695 the *Ouzel Galley*, a merchant ship with a crew of 37 men from Ringsend and nearby Irishtown under Captain Eoghan Massey, set sail from here, bound for Smyrna (now Izmir) in Turkey. When the vessel failed to return after three

years, she was officially declared lost and the insurers compensated her owners. But in 1700, a battered *Ouzel Galley* limped home with a cargo of spices and other exotic goods, a rich haul of pirate loot, and a strange tale to tell. The crew claimed that they had been captured and enslaved by Algerian corsairs, but had eventually managed to take back their ship along with a cargo of pirate booty and make their way home. Was this true? Or had the *Ouzel Galley*, instead of sailing east, turned west to the Caribbean to 'go on the account', as the saying had it, as a pirate? Whatever the truth, neither captain nor crew benefited – the booty went to repay the ship's owners and insurers, and the surplus was used to set up a fund to help bankrupt merchants, while the *Ouzel's* mariners returned to Ringsend to find that their womenfolk had given them up for dead and had found new husbands.

**7** Continue over the junction of Pearse Street (on your right) and MacMahon Bridge. Ahead of you and to

your left, you will see a white cubic building surmounted by a circular glass turret floating on a pontoon moored to the dockside. This is the Waterways Visitor Centre (closed for major refurbishment until mid-2009).

The name of the Grand Canal conjures up visions of Venice, but the reality is more mundane. This was a working canal, built to connect Dublin with the Shannon, Ireland's longest river. Begun in 1755 and completed 41 years later with the opening of the Grand Canal Dock, it was one of the greatest engineering projects of its time, and with the skills learned while building these canals, Irish 'inland navigators' or 'navvies' later worked on great canal projects all over the world. Inside the visitor centre, paintings, photographs and working models demonstrate the history and workings of Ireland's canals and point the way to their future in the 21st century. To return to the city centre, walk to the south end of Grand Canal Quay and turn left to Grand Canal Dock DART station.

# INDEX

# ACKNOWLEDGEMENTS

The Automobile Association would like to thank the following photographers, companies and picture libraries for their assistance in the preparation of this book. Abbreviations for the picture credits are as follows: (AA) AA World Travel Library.

Front Cover: Halfpenny Bridge, SIME/Ripani Massimo/4 Corners Images

3 David Crausby/Alamy; 7 SIME/Ripani Massimo/4 Corners Images; 8 Art Kowalsky/Alamy; 9 AA/Steve Day; 11 The Irish Image Collection/ Axiom; 12 AA/Steve Day; 14 AA/Simon McBride; 17 MS 58 fol.32v Christ with four angels, introductory page to the Gospel of St. Matthew, from the Book of Kells, c.800 © The Board of Trinity College, Dublin, Ireland/The Bridgeman Art Library; 19 AA/Steve Day; 20/21 AA/Simon McBride; 22 The Irish Image Collection/Axiom; 25 AA/Steve Day; 27 AA/Steve Day; 28 Paul Lindsay/Alamy; 31 AA/Steve Day; 32 Stuart Pearson/Fotolibra; 33 AA/Steve Day; 34/35 Jon Arnold/Photolibrary Group; 36 Peter Titmuss/Alamy; 39 Richard Cummins/Lonely Planet Images; 40/41 AA/Steve Day; 42 AA/Steve Day; 43 AA/Steve Day; 45 AA/Steve Day; 46 AA/Steve Day; 48/49 Bruno Barbier/Robert Harding Travel/Photolibrary Group; 50 AA/Steve Day; 51 Paul Mcnamara/Fotolibra; 52 The Irish Image Collection/Photolibrary Group; 54/55 Joe Cornish/Getty Images; 56 Alex Ramsay/Fotolibra; 59 Paul Mcnamara/Fotolibra; 60 AA/Steve Day; 62/63 Brendan Montgomery/Fotolibra; 64 AA/Steve Day; 65 The Irish Image Collection/Photolibrary Group; 67 AA/Stephen Whitehorne; 68 AA/Steve Day; 70 eye35.com/Alamy; 73 AA/Steve Day; 75 The Irish Image Collection/Axiom; 76/77 AA/Steve Day; 78 Nigel B Coates/Fotolibra; 79 Nigel B Coates/Fotolibra; 80 AA/Steve Day; 83 Nigel B Coates/Fotolibra; 84 Profimedia International s.r.o./Alamy; 85 AA/Slide File; 87 AA/Steve Day; 88 AA/Steve Day; 90/91 AA/Steve Day; 92 4Corners/Irek; 95 Alex Ramsay/Fotolibra; 97 Doug McKinlay/Lonely Planet Images; 98 The Irish Image Collection/Photolibrary Group; 100 SIME/Cellai Stefano/4Corners Images; 102 Paul O'kane/Fotolibra; 103 Mark Thomas/Alamy; 104/105 The Irish Image Collection/Axiom; 106 Nigel B Coates/Fotolibra; 107 AA/Steve Day; 109 AA/Steve Day; 110 Adrian Wilson/Beateworks/Corbis; 112 AA/Steve Day; 113 Nigel B Coates/Fotolibra; 115 Neil Setchfield/Alamy; 116 Paul O'kane/Fotolibra; 118/119 Arco Images GmbH/Alamy; 120 AA/Steve Day; 121 Richard Cummins/Lonely Planet Images; 123 AA/Stephen Whitehorne; 124 The Irish Image Collection/Photolibrary Group; 126 AA/Steve Day; 129 Barry Mason/Alamy; 131 AA/Stephen Whitehorne; 132/133 AA/Steve Day; 134 AA/Caroline Jones; 137 AA/Michael Short; 138-139 AA/Caroline Jones; 140 Chris Hill/Scenic Ireland; 141 fstop2/Alamy; 143 Fotolibra; 144 The Irish Image Collection/Photolibrary Group; 146-147 The Irish Image Collection/Photolibrary Group; 148 Nigel B Coates/Fotolibra; 151 Nigel B Coates/Fotolibra; 153 The Irish Image Collection/Photolibrary Group; 154 Nigel B Coates/Fotolibra; 155 Nigel B Coates/Fotolibra; 157 Paul Mcnamara/Fotolibra; 158 Nigel B Coates/ Fotolibra; 160-161 The Irish Image Collection/Axiom; 162 Duncan Maxwell/Robert Harding/Photolibrary Group; 164 Jeremy Woodhouse/ Masterlia; 166 Werner Dieterich/Alamy; 167 AA/Stephen Whitehorne; 168 The Irish Image Collection /Axiom; 171 The Irish Image Collection/ Photolibrary Group; 173 Sylvia Cordaiy Photo Library Ltd/Alamy.

Every effort has been made to trace the copyright holders, and we apologize in advance for any accidental errors. We would be happy to apply the corrections in the following edition of this publication.

# Other titles in the series:

AMSTERDAM — *History & Mystery Walks*

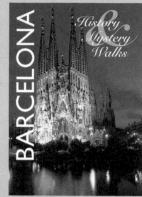

BARCELONA — *History & Mystery Walks*

CHICAGO — *History & Mystery Walks*

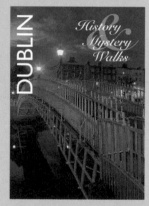

DUBLIN — *History & Mystery Walks*

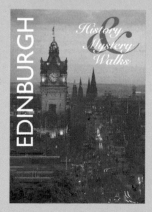

EDINBURGH — *History & Mystery Walks*

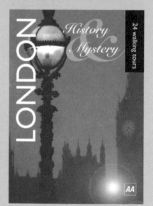

LONDON — *History & Mystery* — 24 walking tours — AA